NEIL MUNRO & IAN STONE

Productivity Unlocked

Master Your Day, Elevate Efficiency, Lead Fearlessly.

Copyright © 2024 by Neil Munro & Ian Stone

©2024 Neil Munro & Ian Stone. All rights reserved. No part of this publication may be reproduced, distributed, or transmitted in any form or by any means, including photocopying, recording, or other electronic or mechanical methods, without the prior written permission of the authors, except in the case of brief quotations embodied in critical reviews and certain other noncommercial uses permitted by copyright law.

The advice and strategies contained herein may not be suitable for every situation. This work is sold with the understanding that the authors and publishers are not engaged in rendering legal, accounting, or other professional services. If professional assistance is required, the services of a competent professional should be sought.

Neither the authors nor the publishers shall be liable for damages arising herefrom. The fact that an individual, organisation, or website is referred to in this work as a citation and/or a potential source of further information does not mean that the authors or the publishers endorse the information the individual, organisation, or website may provide or recommendations they may make. Further, readers should be aware that Internet websites listed in this work may have changed or disappeared between when this work was written and when it is read.

No guarantee is made that you will achieve results similar to those proposed in this book, as previous results do not guarantee a similar outcome. Financial outcomes are based on many factors. No claims or guarantees can be made as to the financial results you will achieve from following the advice set forth in this book. The authors and publishers disclaim any liability, loss, or risk taken by individuals who directly or indirectly act on the information contained herein.

First edition

Contents

	IMPORTANT: READ THIS FIRST	iv
	INTRODUCTION	viii
1	UNLEASHING YOUR INNER PRODUCTIVITY	1
2	RITUALS TO REVOLUTIONISE YOUR ROUTINE	12
3	MASTERING SELF-DISCIPLINE	22
4	OPTIMISING YOUR WORKSPACE	32
5	LEVERAGING TECHNOLOGY FOR PRODUCTIVITY	44
6	BUILDING AND LEADING PRODUCTIVE TEAMS	54
7	MASTERING TIME-BLOCKING AND DELEGATION	65
8	THE ROLE OF CONTINUOUS LEARNING	76
9	BALANCING WORK AND LIFE	86
10	SCALING YOUR SUCCESS	96
11	EMBRACING THE JOURNEY: A CALL TO ACTION	107

IMPORTANT: READ THIS FIRST

Hi, we're Neil Munro and Ian Stone, and we're thrilled you've decided to pick up this book. If you're ready to unlock new levels of productivity and lead with confidence, you've made a smart choice.

With over 20 years of hands-on experience in running businesses from scratch, we've faced countless challenges and misconceptions. These very experiences inspired us to write Productivity Unlocked: Master Your Day, Elevate Efficiency, Lead Fearlessly. This highly regarded book is designed to revolutionise how you approach productivity, leveraging the lessons we've learned and the successes we've achieved throughout our careers.

We understand you may have tried various productivity strategies in the past, only to find them generic, unrelatable, or simply ineffective within your unique business environment. It's discouraging when you invest time and resources, hoping for a transformation, only to be met with disappointment.

Perhaps you've also experienced the frustration of implementing systems that promise efficiency but fail to align with the human element of your business. Creating a schedule is one thing, but inspiring genuine engagement and motivation among your team is an entirely different challenge.

Or maybe you've tried leading without a clear framework for productivity, leaving you feeling more like a firefighter constantly putting out emergencies than a visionary steering a proactive, focused team.

We get it—it's not fair.

The truth is, you're not alone. Many business owners are caught in a cycle of outdated productivity "solutions" that fail to address the root causes of inefficiency or foster sustainable growth.

That feeling of frustration—spinning your wheels without gaining traction, or worse, watching your team disengage because they're not equipped to manage their workload effectively—is far more common than you might think.

Here's what most don't realise: the issue often isn't about working harder but rather about implementing smarter, strategic approaches that align with your business's core goals and the personal aspirations of your team.

With the opportunity to integrate innovative productivity techniques and frameworks, there's no reason for you or your business to remain stuck in a cycle of burnout and underachievement.

Many find themselves in a constant state of anxiety, fearing they're not doing enough or that their efforts won't lead to real-world success. This fear can paralyse even the most ambitious among us, making the path to peak productivity seem unattainable.

But it doesn't have to be this way. Let's embark on this journey together, unlocking the true potential of your daily operations. Let's elevate efficiency and lead with fearless confidence.

The Productivity Paradox Loop

The Productivity Paradox Loop is an endless cycle that traps many business owners and entrepreneurs like you. This vicious loop preys on your desire for greater productivity, both personally and professionally. It promises hope but delivers frustration, leaving you in the same place—or sometimes even further behind. Let's walk through each step of this relentless cycle so you can recognise where you are and understand what lies ahead.

Initial Overwhelm

You wake up bombarded by a never-ending to-do list and an overwhelming sense of responsibility to drive your business forward. Your desk is cluttered with piles of papers, your inbox is overflowing, and you can't seem to find a clear starting point. This chaos not only stifles your productivity but also drains your energy before you even begin. This common trigger point often leads you to seek solutions, but without clear direction, it only deepens the loop.

Fruitless Experimentation

In a bid to regain control, you might experiment with various productivity hacks, tools, or methods you've come across. From time-blocking to a range of apps promising to streamline your workflow, you try them all. Yet, none seem to deliver as promised. Each new tool comes with its own learning curve, often complicating things further. This step leaves you exhausted and disillusioned with the never-ending stream of supposed "solutions."

Temporary Relief

Eventually, you find something that seems to work. A new app or system gives you a glimmer of hope, and for a brief period, your day flows more smoothly. Tasks are getting ticked off; meetings feel less of a chore. However, this relief is often short-lived. The underlying problems in your workflow and time management aren't resolved—they're merely papered over. This deceptive stage can make you believe you've found the answer, but the cracks soon start to show.

Scaling Struggles

Buoyed by this fleeting success, you try to scale these new tools or methods across your business or personal life. Perhaps you introduce them to your team, hoping to multiply the benefits. However, the initial simplicity fades, complexities multiply, and what worked in a small, controlled environment doesn't hold up on a larger scale. This struggle to expand these solutions pulls you deeper into inefficiency, leading to more stress and dissatisfaction.

Illusory Resolution

This final stage in the loop is often the most disheartening. For a moment, everything seems to be running smoothly. You feel like you've cracked the code to productivity. However, as the initial success fades, old problems resurface, and new challenges arise. This realisation hits hard, and you find yourself back at the starting point of the Productivity Paradox Loop.

To achieve true, lasting productivity and avoid the frustration and setbacks, a different approach is essential.

That's why we're so excited you're reading this book. As you turn the page, you'll finally discover the insights and solutions you've been searching for, giving you the tools to break free from the Productivity Paradox Loop for good.

INTRODUCTION

Imagine, for a moment, that you're not just managing your day but mastering it. Picture your productivity not merely improving but optimising to the point where your business doesn't just grow—it scales effortlessly. This isn't about working harder, but working significantly smarter. It's about transforming chaotic energy into a focused force that propels you and your business forward. If this sounds like the vision you have for your future, then you've opened the right book.

In the bustling world of entrepreneurship, where everyone seems to be sprinting in a marathon, it's easy to feel like you're constantly playing catch-up. Yet, what separates the truly successful from the rest isn't just the ability to work hard, but the ability to marshal resources, including time and human capital, in a way that is both efficient and sustainable. This book is crafted to guide you through the process of refining your productivity, ensuring every ounce of your effort counts twice.

Let's begin by discussing the cornerstone of productivity—unleashing your inner potential. This isn't about discovering some hidden reservoir of energy. It's about tapping into the capabilities you already possess and amplifying them. You have the raw materials; now you need the tools to refine them into something truly powerful.

Imagine starting your day with the knowledge that you're going to conquer it. That's not just confidence—it's science. Establishing rituals that not only set the tone but also pace your day can revolutionise your output. These aren't simply morning routines; they're strategically placed rituals that serve as checkpoints, keeping you focused and productive throughout your day.

Self-discipline often has a negative connotation, sometimes seen as a form of punishment. But here, we're turning that notion on its head. Mastering self-discipline means mastering freedom—the freedom to make choices that align perfectly with your goals. It's about making disciplined choices so consistently that they become second nature, reducing the mental load that comes with decision-making.

Moving from the internal to the external, let's consider your environment. Optimising your workspace goes beyond ergonomic chairs and standing desks. It's about creating an environment that primes you both psychologically and physically for peak performance. Whether you work in a bustling office or a quiet corner of your home, how your space is designed can dramatically affect your output.

Technology is your lever in the world of productivity. The right tools can automate mundane tasks, giving you back hours in your day. It's not just about using technology, but mastering it so that it works for you, not against you. From simple automation tools to comprehensive project management systems, the right technology stack can act as a force multiplier for your business's efficiency.

But what's a leader without a team? Building and leading productive teams isn't just about hiring the right people; it's about inspiring them to perform at their best. This section of your journey focuses on fostering a culture where productivity is the norm, not the exception. In this environment, productivity isn't enforced—it's inspired.

Mastering time-blocking and delegation is all about owning your time—arguably your most valuable resource. Here, you'll learn not just to manage or spend time, but to invest it wisely. Time-blocking isn't simply a scheduling tool; it's a strategic approach that ensures your most important tasks receive the attention they deserve.

Continuous learning keeps you at the cutting edge, not just in market trends or technological advancements, but in evolving as a leader. Stagnation is the enemy of growth, and in a world that's changing faster than ever, learning is your lifeline.

Balancing work and life might sound like a tired phrase, but here's a fresh perspective. It's not about working less; it's about bringing more life into your work. It's about finding passion and purpose in what you do so that work and life aren't two opposing forces, but parts of a harmonious whole.

Finally, scaling your success isn't just about bigger numbers, a wider reach, or greater profits. It's about scaling sustainably and smartly, in a way that doesn't sacrifice your values, your team's well-being, or your own peace of mind.

This book isn't just a manual; it's a catalyst for transforming not only how you work but how you live. It's about unlocking the most powerful version of yourself, leading fearlessly, and setting benchmarks that lead to meaningful growth. Let's dive in and embark on this transformative journey together.

1

UNLEASHING YOUR INNER PRODUCTIVITY

"Productivity is never an accident. It is always the result of a commitment to excellence, intelligent planning, and focused effort."
— Paul J. Meyer

The Foundations of Productive Mindset

Embarking on the journey of enhanced productivity starts with a solid foundation. As a business owner or entrepreneur, you already know that the mindset with which you approach your day can either set you up for success or hold you back. Let's dive into how you can construct a robust mental framework that will prime you for efficiency and leadership.

Understanding Cognitive Biases

Your brain, brilliant as it is, can sometimes be a bit of a trickster. Cognitive biases, the subtle artifices of your mind, can distort your perception of reality, affecting your decisions and actions. Recognising these biases is the first step in overcoming them, ensuring they don't interfere with your productivity.

One common bias is the **confirmation bias**, where you might favour information that confirms your pre-existing beliefs. This can be particularly limiting when exploring new business strategies or solutions. To counteract this, actively seek out information and viewpoints that challenge your assumptions. It might be uncomfortable, but it's often where the biggest breakthroughs happen.

Another significant bias is the **sunk cost fallacy**. You've probably faced it before: continuing a project or task just because you've already invested a lot into it, not because it's the best decision moving forward. Here's a Ferris-approved tip: consistently evaluate your tasks and projects with a fresh perspective. Ask yourself, "If I wasn't already involved, would I enter into this now?" If the answer is no, it might be time to cut your losses and redirect your energy.

By understanding and managing these biases, you create a clearer path for decision-making, one that's based on current and relevant information rather than skewed perceptions.

The Power of Positive Thinking

Now, let's talk about the muscle of your mind: positive thinking. It sounds a bit cliché, right? But here's the twist: positive thinking isn't about expecting the best to happen every time but accepting that whatever happens is the best for that moment. It's a powerful tool for resilience and motivation.

Imagine you're pitching a new product or service, and the response isn't what you hoped for. A negative mindset might spiral into self-doubt or blame, which stalls productivity. On the flip side, a positive mindset prompts you to extract valuable insights from the experience and pivot quickly. It's about leveraging every outcome as a stepping stone towards your goals.

To cultivate this mindset, start your day with a positivity ritual. It could be as simple as writing down three things you're grateful for or affirmations that reinforce your capabilities and goals. Over time, this practice can shift your default mental state to one that's more optimistic and energised, setting a positive tone for the day's work.

Cultivating Mental Clarity

Mental clarity is about having a lucid understanding of what you want to achieve and the steps required to get there. This clarity can dramatically enhance your productivity by aligning your daily actions with your broader business objectives.

Begin by decluttering your mental space. Just as you would tidy up your physical workspace to foster productivity, your mental environment needs regular tidying up too. Dedicate time to reflect on your current projects and responsibilities. Identify any tasks that might be creating noise rather than value, and have the courage to delegate or drop them.

Another effective strategy is meditation. It's been embraced by many top entrepreneurs for its benefits in improving focus, reducing stress, and maintaining mental health. Even a few minutes a day can help clear the mental fog, allowing you to see your business and your role within it more clearly.

Lastly, keep the communication lines open with your team. A shared vision and clear objectives not only enhance collective clarity but also drive individual and group productivity. Ensure everyone is on the same page and watch how quickly things start moving forward.

By building a productive mindset grounded in an understanding of cognitive biases, the habit of positive thinking, and the pursuit of mental clarity, you equip yourself with the mental tools necessary for leading effectively and efficiently. As you continue to apply these principles, you'll notice not just incremental but exponential improvements in how you manage and grow your business. It all starts in the mind, after all.

Time Management Essentials

Mastering the art of time management is akin to acquiring a superpower, especially for you, the entrepreneur who juggles countless tasks daily. The essence of effective time management lies in three critical areas: prioritisation techniques, tools for scheduling, and overcoming procrastination. Let's dive into each of these components to help you streamline your day and maximise your productivity.

Prioritisation Techniques

Understanding how to prioritise tasks is fundamental in managing your time efficiently. One effective method is the Eisenhower Box, also known as the Urgent-Important Matrix. This tool helps you visualise and decide on which tasks to focus on immediately, which to schedule for later, which to delegate, and which to drop entirely. The matrix is divided into four quadrants:- Urgent and important (tasks you will do immediately).- Important, but not urgent (tasks you will schedule to do later).- Urgent, but not important (tasks you will delegate to someone else).- Neither urgent nor important (tasks you will eliminate).

The beauty of this technique lies in its simplicity and the clarity it provides in decision-making. By categorising tasks based on their urgency and importance, you can fight the all-too-common entrepreneurial fire-fighting mode and focus on what truly moves the needle for your business.

Another prioritisation strategy is the Pareto Principle, or the 80/20 rule, which suggests that 80% of outcomes result from 20% of all causes. In a business context, this might mean that 80% of your sales come from 20% of your clients. Identifying these critical 20% tasks and focusing your energy there can dramatically increase your effectiveness without necessarily increasing your workload.

Tools for Scheduling

With priorities clearly identified, the next step is to organise them into a manageable schedule. Today's technology offers a plethora of tools designed to streamline this process, each with unique features tailored to different types of users and businesses.

For instance, Google Calendar is a widely used tool that allows you to colour-code different types of activities and set reminders for upcoming appointments. This can be especially useful for visually oriented individuals. If you're someone who manages a team, project management tools like Asana or Trello can help keep track of both your schedule and that of your team, ensuring everyone is aligned and on task.

For those who prefer a more holistic view of their time, time blocking can be a very effective strategy. This involves dividing your day into blocks of time and assigning specific tasks to each block. Not only does this help in maintaining focus on the task at hand, but it also limits the time spent on each task, pushing you to work more efficiently.

One often overlooked aspect of scheduling is the need for breaks. Tools like the Pomodoro Technique, which involves working for focused intervals (typically 25 minutes) followed by short breaks (5 minutes), can significantly enhance productivity. This method helps in maintaining high levels of concentration while preventing burnout.

Overcoming Procrastination

Procrastination is the arch-nemesis of productivity. It's the habit of delaying tasks that need to be done, often in favour of less urgent, more pleasurable activities. Overcoming this can be challenging, but with the right strategies, it is certainly manageable.

One effective way to combat procrastination is by setting clear, actionable steps for each task. Often, tasks can seem daunting because they are too vague or monumental. By breaking them down into smaller, manageable steps, the task becomes less intimidating and easier to start.

Another technique is the Five Minute Miracle, where you commit to working on a task for just five minutes. Often, starting is the hardest part, and once you've begun, it's easier to keep going. This method helps bypass the initial resistance and builds momentum.

Lastly, hold yourself accountable. Whether it's through a mentor, a business coach, or a peer accountability group, having someone to answer to can provide the extra push needed to get moving. Regular check-ins can also help you monitor your progress and recalibrate as needed.

Incorporating these time management essentials into your routine requires commitment and continual refinement. As you become more adept at prioritising, scheduling, and overcoming procrastination, you'll notice significant strides in your ability to manage the day effectively. These skills not only enhance your productivity but also free up time to focus on strategic growth and personal development—key areas that drive business success and personal fulfilment.

Setting Achievable Goals

When you're knee-deep in the bustling life of entrepreneurship, setting goals is much like plotting a roadmap through uncharted territory. It's the strategic design that guides you from one milestone to the next, ensuring that each step you take is calculated and effective. By adopting a structured approach to your goal-setting, you not only magnify your chances of success but also enhance your productivity by keeping you focused and motivated. Let's break down this process into manageable parts, starting with S.M.A.R.T goal setting.

S.M.A.R.T Goal Setting

You've likely heard of S.M.A.R.T goals before—Specific, Measurable, Achievable, Relevant, and Time-bound. While it might sound like just another acronym, these five characteristics are crucial in crafting goals that are not only clear but also attainable.

Begin by being Specific. Instead of setting a goal like "increase business revenue," define exactly how much increase you are aiming for—say, a 20% increase in yearly revenue. This clarity eliminates ambiguity and sets a clear target.

Next, ensure your goals are Measurable. By quantifying your goals, you create markers that can be assessed. In our example of increasing revenue, decide how you will measure this growth. Will it be through monthly sales reports or quarterly profit analyses?

The third characteristic, Achievable, requires you to be realistic. There's a fine balance between setting a challenging goal and setting yourself up for failure. If your business is still in its infancy, a 20% revenue increase might be overambitious. Adjust your targets to align with the realistic growth patterns typical for your industry and current economic conditions.

Relevance is your fourth criterion. Your goals need to align with your broader business objectives and values. If your primary aim is to enhance customer satisfaction, then focusing solely on revenue might divert resources and energy from initiatives that directly improve customer service.

Lastly, make your goals Time-bound. This involves setting a deadline which compels you to prioritise and manage your time effectively. For our revenue increase goal, you might set a timeframe of one year. This deadline can help motivate your team and give you a clear timeline for measuring progress.

Milestones and Checkpoints

With your S.M.A.R.T goals in place, the next step is to establish milestones and checkpoints. These are like the signposts along your journey that confirm you're heading in the right direction. They break down your larger goal into smaller, more manageable parts, making the process less daunting and more achievable.

For instance, if your goal is to increase annual revenue by 20%, set quarterly milestones of 5% revenue growth. Each quarter acts as a checkpoint where you can evaluate your progress, analyse what's working and what isn't, and make necessary adjustments. This periodic assessment helps maintain your momentum and adapt strategies in real-time, ensuring that you're always on the most effective path towards your ultimate objective.

Moreover, celebrating these smaller victories can significantly boost morale, both for you and your team. It reinforces the belief that the larger goal is within reach and that every effort is contributing towards that end.

Visualising Success

Finally, while this might seem like a softer aspect of goal setting, visualising success is a powerful tool that can significantly impact your psychological state and drive. Visualisation is the process of creating a mental image of your desired outcome, imagining having already achieved your goals.

Engage in this practice regularly, perhaps at the start of your day or during a break. Picture yourself signing a lucrative client contract, seeing a significant profit margin on your financial sheets, or celebrating a milestone achievement. What does it look like? How do you feel? Who is with you? The more vividly you can imagine these scenarios, the more real they become in your subconscious mind.

This technique not only enhances motivation but also prepares you mentally to face the challenges along the way. It builds a resilience and confidence that what you are striving for is not only possible but almost tangible.

By incorporating these three components into your goal-setting strategy, you establish a robust framework that supports not just the achievement of your goals but also enhances your overall productivity and efficiency. S.M.A.R.T goals give you a clear and structured path, milestones and checkpoints keep you aligned and motivated, and visualising success ensures that you remain emotionally connected and resilient throughout your entrepreneurial journey. Each of these elements intertwines to form a comprehensive approach that not only outlines what you want to achieve but also empowers you to get there.

RECAP AND ACTION ITEMS

Congratulations on reaching this point. You've just armed yourself with essential strategies to unlock a productivity powerhouse within you. Remember, the journey towards enhanced productivity is both rewarding and continuous. Let's briefly recap what you've covered and dive into some practical steps you can take today to start seeing real changes.

Firstly, you've tackled the Foundations of a Productive Mindset by understanding cognitive biases, embracing the power of positive thinking, and cultivating mental clarity. These elements are crucial as they lay the groundwork for a resilient and focused mind. To implement this, begin each morning by identifying thoughts that might be clouding your judgement or holding you back, and actively reframe them to serve your goals better.

Moving on to Time Management Essentials, you explored prioritisation techniques, tools for scheduling, and methods to overcome procrastination. The key here is to put these into practice by planning your week every Sunday evening. Use digital tools like calendar apps to block out time for high-priority tasks, and set clear deadlines for each project phase.

Lastly, in Setting Achievable Goals, you learned about S.M.A.R.T goal setting, the importance of milestones and checkpoints, and the power of visualising success. Start by writing down one major goal for the next quarter using the S.M.A.R.T framework. Break this goal into smaller, manageable tasks with specific milestones, and take a few minutes daily to visualise achieving this goal and the steps involved.

Here are your action steps:

1. Each morning, spend five minutes identifying and reframing any negative or limiting thoughts

2. Plan your week every Sunday, prioritising tasks that align with your strategic goals, and use tools to keep you on track

3. Set a S.M.A.R.T goal for the next quarter, break it down into actionable steps, and regularly visualise your success.

By consistently applying these strategies, you'll find yourself not only working more efficiently but also leading with greater clarity and confidence. Remember, productivity isn't just about doing more; it's about creating more impact with less stress. So, take these steps, make them habitual, and watch as your day, and eventually your business, transforms into the model of efficiency and effectiveness you aspire to achieve.

2

RITUALS TO REVOLUTIONISE YOUR ROUTINE

"Productivity is never an accident. It is always the result of a commitment to excellence, intelligent planning, and focused effort."
— Paul J. Meyer

Morning Rituals

Imagine starting your day not just on the right foot, but with a sprint down the path of peak productivity and sharp mental clarity. For business owners and entrepreneurs like you, mornings aren't just the start of a new day; they are the launchpad for success. Here's how you can architect a morning that sets you up to conquer the business world.

The Miracle Morning

The concept of a 'Miracle Morning' has been a game-changer for many successful entrepreneurs. The idea is simple yet profound: dedicate the first hour of your day to activities that nurture your personal growth and mental wellbeing. This isn't about checking emails or scrolling through social media. It's about giving yourself a structured start that fuels both your mind and body, preparing you to tackle the day's challenges with vigour.

Start by waking up just one hour earlier than usual. Yes, it might feel a bit brutal at first, especially if you're a night owl, but the benefits are worth it. Use this time to engage in activities that you wouldn't otherwise fit into your hectic day. This could include reading, writing, exercising, or any practice that enhances your personal development and sense of well-being.

Why does this matter? As an entrepreneur, you're constantly reacting to the demands of the world around you. The Miracle Morning gives you space to proactively cultivate the qualities you need to respond to these demands effectively, such as resilience, focus, and creativity.

Exercise as a Keystone Habit

Charles Duhigg, in his book The Power of Habit, introduces the idea of keystone habits. These are habits that, once adopted, can trigger widespread changes in behaviour. For many successful individuals, regular exercise is precisely that—a keystone habit that sets the stage for other good habits and mindsets.

Incorporating exercise into your morning routine doesn't mean you need to run a marathon every day. It's about consistency and movement. Even 20 minutes of physical activity, be it yoga, a brisk walk, or a quick HIIT session, can elevate your mood and energy levels, sharpen your focus, and improve your health.

The science backs this up too. Exercise releases endorphins, often referred to as the body's feel-good hormones. It also helps to regulate other neurotransmitters, like dopamine and serotonin, which play a crucial role in mood and motivation.

For you, the busy entrepreneur, morning exercise can transform your entire day. Not only does it boost your energy levels, but it also helps to clear your mind, making you more effective in making decisions and solving problems. Think of your morning workout as priming your brain for success.

Meditation and Mindfulness

In the hustle and bustle of running a business, it's easy to get swept up in the never-ending to-do list and the stress that comes with it. This is where meditation and mindfulness can be transformative, particularly if practised first thing in the morning.

Meditation, in its simplest form, involves sitting quietly and paying attention to your breath. When your mind wanders, as it will, you gently bring your focus back to your breathing. Just ten minutes each morning can significantly impact your day, helping you reduce stress, enhance concentration, and increase overall emotional resilience.

Mindfulness, while related to meditation, involves maintaining a moment-by-moment awareness of our thoughts, feelings, bodily sensations, and the surrounding environment. It's about being present and fully engaged with whatever we're doing at the moment — free from distraction or judgement.

Why should you care? As an entrepreneur, you're likely familiar with the level of stress and the multitude of tasks demanding your attention. By starting your day with meditation and mindfulness, you equip yourself to maintain calm and focus amidst the chaos. It's about training your mind to be less reactive to stress and more responsive to the demands of your business.

Integrating these practices into your morning doesn't just help you manage stress; it enhances your ability to concentrate, think creatively, and interact with your clients and team with a clear, focused mind.

By revolutionising your mornings with these rituals — The Miracle Morning, Exercise as a Keystone Habit, and Meditation and Mindfulness — you're not just preparing for the day ahead. You are setting a foundation for lifelong success, health, and well-being. This isn't just about surviving another day; it's about thriving as an entrepreneur and leading your business to new heights. So, set your alarm, lace up your trainers, and prepare to greet the day with enthusiasm and a clear mind. Your empire awaits.

Workday Rituals

Managing energy, not time, is an approach that might initially sound counterintuitive, particularly in a culture obsessed with squeezing every drop out of the available hours. Yet, as an entrepreneur, you know the value of peak performance, and that's rarely sustained by merely watching the clock. The traditional model pushes for longer hours, but let's flip that perspective: focus on maximising your energy for high-impact activities. This is about working smarter, not harder.

Consider your body a bit like a smartphone battery. Start the day at 100%, and each task drains a bit of power. Some tasks are like those power-hungry apps; they drain your energy faster than others. Your job is to manage your energy reserves so you don't hit that dreaded red zone by midday.

Firstly, identify your high-energy periods. Most people have a spike in the morning, shortly after they start their day, and perhaps another in the late afternoon. These are your golden hours. Schedule your most demanding tasks during these times – those requiring strategic thinking, creativity, or important decision making. Save the low-energy-demand tasks, like checking emails or administrative chores, for when your energy starts to dip.

Next, consciously fuel your energy levels throughout the day. This isn't just about what you eat and drink (although stabilising your blood sugar by choosing snacks and meals wisely is crucial). It's also about what you consume mentally and emotionally. Minimise interactions that drain your energy – yes, we all have those! Instead, try to engage with people and tasks that invigorate and inspire you. Sometimes a quick chat with a supportive colleague or a brisk walk outside can recharge your batteries.

Now, let's talk about the role of breaks. It's tempting to barrel through the day without pause, especially when the to-do list looks daunting. But here's a secret that highly productive people know: taking regular breaks is not a sign of slacking off; it's an investment in sustained productivity. Breaks reduce mental fatigue, boost brain function, and maintain performance throughout the day without the typical late-afternoon crash.

The key to effective breaks is to be intentional. It's not just about stopping work; it's about refreshing your mind and body. A five-minute break every hour can prevent burnout. Stretch, move around, or do something completely unrelated to work. Practice deep breathing or a quick meditation. These activities can significantly lower stress levels, leading to clearer thinking and better problem-solving when you return to work.

Moreover, ever noticed how some tasks just naturally cluster together? That's where batch processing comes into play. It's a method where similar tasks are performed consecutively without interruption. This approach leverages the principle that similar tasks require similar resources, whether mental or physical, thus reducing the start-up and slow-down time needed when switching between different types of tasks.

Batch processing is particularly effective in managing routine tasks like email, phone calls, and meetings. Instead of letting emails interrupt your workflow throughout the day, try setting specific times to handle them. Perhaps once in mid-morning and once late afternoon. Apply the same method to other routine tasks. By batching, you reduce the context-switching that can eat away at your efficiency.

For instance, if social media is part of your business strategy, don't check it sporadically. Set a time for social media activities and stick to it. Use tools that allow you to schedule posts in advance. This not only helps in maintaining consistency across your channels but also frees you up to focus on other tasks without distraction.

In applying these strategies—managing your energy wisely, taking smart breaks, and batching similar tasks—you'll find that your workday not only becomes more productive but also less exhausting. You'll leave the office feeling accomplished, not drained, with energy reserves to enjoy your personal life after hours.

By shifting focus from clock-watching to energy management, embracing the rejuvenating power of breaks, and optimising task handling through batch processing, you revolutionise your workday. These aren't just tweaks to your routine; they're transformative practices that can lead to significant gains in productivity and satisfaction. Embrace them, and watch as your days transform, enabling you to lead more effectively and fearlessly.

Evening Rituals

Unwinding for Success

As the sun dips below the horizon and the day's hustle begins to quiet, your opportunity to set the stage for tomorrow takes shape. Unwinding isn't merely about relaxing; it's about strategically disengaging to ensure that you're recharged and ready for another day of high performance.

Begin by creating an environment that signals to your brain that work is over. This might mean shutting down your computer, turning off notifications, or even changing into more comfortable clothing. These signals help transition your mind from a state of high alert to a mode of relaxation.

Next, consider incorporating activities that decrease your cortisol levels—the stress hormone that can keep you wired and hinder sleep. Gentle physical activities such as yoga or a leisurely walk can be immensely beneficial. Yoga, in particular, combines physical movement with mindfulness, aiding both your body and mind to unwind.

Moreover, visualisation techniques can be incredibly powerful in this phase. Spend a few minutes visualising your ideal next day, focusing on the feelings of success and the completion of goals. This not only helps in relaxation but also primes your subconscious to tackle the challenges that lie ahead.

Remember, the key is consistency. Establishing a routine that helps you transition from the intensity of your entrepreneurial day into a restful evening is crucial for long-term success. This doesn't mean your routine should be rigid or void of relaxation. On the contrary, it should be something you look forward to—a period of calm and enjoyment that enhances your overall wellbeing.

Planning the Next Day

Once you've begun to decompress, it's time to briefly turn your attention to the day ahead. This isn't about diving deep into work tasks again, but rather, about setting clear intentions so you can hit the ground running in the morning without any guesswork.

Start with a simple list. What are the top three priorities for tomorrow? These should be tasks that will have the most significant impact on your goals. Resist the urge to over-plan. Overloading your agenda can lead to stress and a feeling of overwhelm before the day even begins. Instead, focus on what's truly important—what will move the needle in your business?

Utilise tools that resonate with you. Some entrepreneurs find benefit in digital tools and apps designed to organise tasks and manage time effectively.

Others prefer the tangibility of writing in a planner or journal. Whatever your preference, ensure it is something that you can consistently adhere to.

Time-blocking can also be an effective strategy here. Allocate specific blocks of time for deep work, meetings, and personal time. This method not only helps in prioritising tasks but also in maintaining a healthy work-life balance, which is crucial for sustained productivity and creativity.

Reflective Journaling

The final piece of your evening ritual is reflective journaling. This isn't about documenting every detail of your day, but rather, reflecting on the progress towards your goals, the lessons learned, and how you can improve.

Ask yourself some key questions: What went well today? What didn't? How did I handle stress and setbacks? Is there something I could do better? This kind of reflection fosters a growth mindset, helping you to see challenges as opportunities for learning and development.

Keep this practice brief; about five to ten minutes should suffice. The aim is to gain insights and closure from the day's work, not to dwell on what didn't go as planned. This practice should be constructive and uplifting, steering your mind towards positivity and readiness for the new day.

Incorporate gratitude as well. List at least three things you are thankful for from the day. Gratitude shifts your focus from what's lacking to what's abundant, promoting a positive mindset and reducing stress.

By making reflective journaling a non-negotiable part of your evening, you develop a powerful tool for self-awareness and continuous improvement. This routine not only enhances your personal growth but also impacts your business positively, as you start each day with a clear, focused, and optimistic mindset.

Establishing effective evening rituals is as crucial as how you start your day. They provide a perfect bookend to your busy schedule, allowing you to unwind, plan ahead, and reflect. As an entrepreneur, your days are filled with decisions, challenges, and constant demands on your energy. By investing time in evening rituals, you ensure that you manage not just your business, but also your most valuable asset—yourself. With these practices, you create not just a routine, but a lifestyle that supports sustained success and wellbeing.

RECAP AND ACTION ITEMS

You've now explored a comprehensive suite of rituals designed to revolutionise your daily routine, from the moment you wake to the minute you close your eyes at night. It's time to put these concepts into practice and see how they can elevate your productivity, efficiency, and overall leadership.

Morning Rituals: Kickstart your day with purpose. Tomorrow, rise a bit earlier and dedicate the first hour to The Miracle Morning. Engage in at least 20 minutes of physical activity to awaken your body and mind. Follow this with a meditation session to clear your mental clutter and focus on the day ahead.

Workday Rituals: Think of your energy as a more critical metric than time. Start by categorising your tasks and batching similar ones together, reducing the start-stop energy expenditure. Intersperse these batches with short, planned breaks to recharge—step outside, stretch, or do a quick mindfulness exercise.

Evening Rituals: Wind down effectively by setting a consistent routine that helps transition your mind from work to rest. Reflect on your day with a journal, noting successes and areas for improvement. Plan tomorrow's tasks tonight. This not only sets your agenda but also aids in closing mental loops so you can rest without work invading your thoughts.

Action Steps:

1. **Implement Gradually:** Don't overhaul your life overnight. Incorporate one new ritual from each section per week

2. **Monitor and Adjust:** Keep a log of how each change affects your productivity and wellbeing. Tweak as necessary

3. **Stay Consistent:** It takes time to form new habits. Commit to these rituals for at least 21 days before making any judgments

4. **Seek Feedback:** Discuss these changes with peers or a mentor. They can provide insights and accountability.

Remember, the goal isn't just to work harder but smarter. By optimising your routine through these targeted rituals, you're setting yourself up to lead more effectively and fearlessly. Let these revamped routines be the backbone of your day, supporting you as you stride towards greater achievements.

3

MASTERING SELF-DISCIPLINE

"We are what we repeatedly do. Excellence, then, is not an act, but a habit." - Aristotle

Understanding Self-Discipline

Delving into self-discipline isn't merely about tightening your schedule or filling every minute of your day with productivity hacks. It's about understanding the intricate dance between your mind's desires and your long-term goals. For you, the driven entrepreneur, mastering this can be the linchpin in your journey from being good to being truly great.

The Psychology Behind Self-Control

At its core, self-control is your ability to regulate impulses so that you stay aligned with long-term goals rather than succumbing to short-term temptations. It's what makes you skip the seduction of the 'snooze' button in favour of rising early to strategise your day's work. But why is this a Herculean feat for many?

The brain's prefrontal cortex, where self-control is managed, is like a muscle. Just as your biceps tire out after repeated curls, your self-control depletes with overuse. Each decision you make, from choosing a healthy lunch to deciding on a client proposal, chips away at your willpower.

Cognitive psychologists refer to this phenomenon as 'ego depletion'. The theory suggests that willpower isn't an infinite well we can draw from but a battery that needs recharging through rest, a nourishing diet, and positive social interactions. Understanding this can dramatically shift how you structure your day. Prioritise tasks that require the highest level of self-discipline when your battery is fully charged, typically after a good night's sleep or following a restful break.

Common Pitfalls

As an entrepreneur, you're no stranger to pitfalls; they are part and parcel of the business landscape. However, when it comes to self-discipline, certain common traps can derail even the most determined amongst us.

Overcommitment is a frequent misstep. In your zeal to chase down every opportunity, you might find yourself stretched thinner than a start-up's budget. This dilutes your energy and, crucially, your self-control reserves. Learn to say no, or at least, not right now.

Misaligned goals also play a part. If your day-to-day activities aren't lined up with your overarching visions, each task becomes a boulder you must push uphill. Aligning your goals effectively acts like greasing the slope, making discipline less about enduring pain and more about enjoying progress.

Lastly, **underestimating the power of stress** to erode your self-discipline is a critical oversight. Stress triggers the brain's fight or flight response, diverting energy away from the prefrontal cortex, thus impairing your ability to make thoughtful, disciplined decisions. Managing stress isn't a luxury; it's essential for maintaining the self-discipline necessary to achieve your business goals.

Building Willpower

Building willpower is akin to building a muscle. It requires consistent practice and the right techniques. Here's how you can strengthen yours:

Start small. If you aspire to work a solid ten-hour day, begin by ensuring you can productively manage one hour, then two, and so on. Small victories compile to build confidence and reinforce your willpower.

Establish clear, achievable goals. Ambiguity is the enemy of self-discipline. The clearer your goals, the easier it is to commit to actions that help achieve them. Instead of "increase revenue," set a specific target: "increase revenue by 20% in six months through upselling current clients and acquiring new leads."

Practice mindfulness. Mindfulness teaches you to observe your thoughts and feelings without judgement. This awareness creates a gap between impulses and actions, allowing you to choose responses that align with your goals rather than being hijacked by momentary desires.

Strengthen your willpower with routine. Willpower is highest in the morning for most people, so start your day with tasks that require the most self-control. Protect this time from distractions. As you repeat this pattern, it becomes a routine, reducing the mental load required to make decisions.

Entrepreneurs like you thrive on the thrill of turning visions into reality. However, without the bedrock of self-discipline, sustaining success is akin to building a skyscraper on sand. By understanding the psychology of self-control, recognising common pitfalls, and actively building your willpower, you equip yourself not just to meet challenges but to anticipate and prepare for them, keeping your business vision sharp and your journey forward relentless.

Strategies for Staying on Track

Accountability Systems

In the realm of entrepreneurship, where self-motivation is paramount, accountability systems are not just helpful; they are essential. Consider the structure of an accountability system as a framework that keeps you aligned with your goals, especially when the initial spark of inspiration dims. It's like having a co-pilot in your entrepreneurial journey, one that ensures you're always on course.

The first step in establishing a robust accountability system is to set clear, actionable goals. These aren't just any goals, but ones that are specific, measurable, attainable, relevant, and time-bound (SMART). Once your goals are set, the next phase is to share them. This could be with a business partner, a mentor, or even a peer group. The act of sharing your goals not only makes them more real but also puts a bit of healthy pressure on you to meet them.

Furthermore, regular check-ins are crucial. Whether it's a weekly meeting with a business coach or a daily catch-up with your team, these check-ins compel you to reflect on your progress and confront the areas where you're lagging. Digital tools and apps designed for tracking progress can also play a significant role here, providing a visual representation of your progress and areas needing attention.

Lastly, do not underestimate the power of a mastermind group. This is a gathering of like-minded individuals who challenge each other to set powerful goals, and more importantly, to accomplish them. Each member's involvement generates a synergy that boosts the individual and collective performance. By being part of such a group, you not only gain fresh perspectives on your challenges but also benefit from an elevated level of mutual support and encouragement.

Reward and Punishment

The carrot and stick approach has been used for centuries in various forms, and its application in self-discipline is profoundly effective. Applying this concept involves setting up rewards for achievement and penalties for failures, which could significantly boost your drive and commitment.

Start by identifying rewards that genuinely motivate you. It could be as simple as a weekend getaway after completing a significant project or treating yourself to a fine dining experience after meeting a sales target. The key is to ensure that the reward is desirable enough to spur you forward. For an entrepreneur, time is often more valuable than money, so rewards that offer relaxation and rejuvenation can be particularly effective.

On the flip side, establish penalties for not meeting your commitments. This might involve financial penalties, such as donating to a charity for each deadline missed or personal penalties like losing the privilege to watch your favourite TV show. It's crucial that these penalties are impactful enough to motivate you to avoid them but not so harsh that they're debilitating.

Incorporating this system requires self-honesty above all. You need to be willing to enforce these rewards and punishments on yourself, which is not always easy. It calls for a rigorous self-assessment and the ability to hold oneself accountable without external enforcement.

Environmental Control

Your environment can significantly influence your ability to stay disciplined. As an entrepreneur, you often have the autonomy to shape your environment, so why not design it to bolster your productivity?

Firstly, consider your physical workspace. It should be organised and conducive to work. This might mean decluttering your desk, investing in a comfortable chair, or setting up adequate lighting. The fewer distractions you have within your immediate vicinity, the more focused you will be.

Next, think about the digital environment. With the bulk of entrepreneurial work happening on digital devices, it's essential to streamline your digital space. Organise your files, set up efficient workflows, and use tools that enhance productivity. Moreover, limiting notifications and setting boundaries around email checking can significantly reduce digital distractions.

Lastly, examine your social environment. The people around you can either lift you up or bring you down. Surround yourself with supportive individuals who inspire and motivate you. This might involve distancing yourself from negative influences or spending more time with people who share your aspirations and work ethic.

By controlling these aspects of your environment, you create a space that naturally enhances your self-discipline. It's about making the path to productive work the path of least resistance.

In conclusion, staying on track isn't just about having an iron will; it's about smartly leveraging tools and techniques that align your daily actions with your long-term goals. Accountability systems keep you honest, reward and punishment schemes keep you motivated, and a controlled environment keeps you focused. Together, they form a coherent strategy that can dramatically elevate your productivity and efficiency.

Long-Term Discipline

Habit stacking, the compound effect, and renewing commitment are not just concepts; they are powerful tools that can dramatically alter the trajectory of your entrepreneurial journey. By understanding and implementing these strategies, you lay down the framework for sustained productivity and efficiency, crucial for anyone leading a venture. These tools are about creating a self-disciplined lifestyle that supports your long-term business goals and personal aspirations.

Habit Stacking

The concept of habit stacking may sound simple, but its implications are profound. In essence, habit stacking involves grouping together small activities into a single routine that you perform consistently. For instance, instead of just setting your alarm to wake up, stack it with immediate actions like making your bed, a five-minute meditation, and writing a quick to-do list for the day. The beauty of this approach lies in its simplicity and the compound effect it creates over time.

For you, as a business owner, think about the daily tasks that contribute to your enterprise's success. Perhaps it's checking the financial health of your business, engaging with your team, or reviewing customer feedback. By stacking these habits, you create a non-negotiable routine that powers your day. It's about making those critical tasks as habitual as brushing your teeth – automatic and non-negotiable.

Implementing habit stacking requires you to identify key activities that yield high returns and chaining them together in a sequence that you follow religiously. The trick is to start small. Choose habits that are manageable and directly impactful to your productivity and efficiency. Over time, these small actions accumulate, leading to significant achievements without the constant battle of decision-making and procrastination.

The Compound Effect

The compound effect is essentially the principle that small, consistent actions can lead to significant outcomes over time. In the context of self-discipline, it means that every small decision and action contributes to a larger impact in your life and business. It's the repeated routine of your daily discipline that builds the foundations of your entrepreneurial success.

Consider this: if you improve your efficiency by just 1% every day, those small gains compound into a notable increase in overall productivity over a year. For an entrepreneur, this might mean dedicating time each day to read industry news, refine your business strategy, or expand your network. These tasks might seem trivial on a day-to-day basis but compounded over time, they significantly enhance your understanding and operation of your business.

To leverage the compound effect, you must remain consistent with your efforts, no matter how small they are. Skipping a day here and there might not seem like much, but it disrupts the compounding progress. Maintaining discipline in the small tasks ensures you are always moving towards your larger goals, even if the steps seem incremental at the moment.

Renewing Commitment

Staying disciplined over the long haul requires you to continually renew your commitment to your goals. This renewal is vital, as it's easy to lose sight of the bigger picture when caught up in day-to-day operations. Renewal doesn't necessarily mean making huge changes; rather, it involves regular reflection on your progress, goals, and the strategies you are employing to reach them.

Set aside time each week or month to review your achievements and setbacks. This reflection allows you to stay aligned with your long-term objectives and adjust your strategies as needed. Remember, flexibility is a component of discipline. As your business evolves, so too should your habits and routines.

Renewing your commitment can also mean reaffirming your 'why' – the reason you started your business in the first place. It could be a personal ambition, a desire to make an impact, or a drive towards financial independence. Whatever it is, reconnecting with your 'why' can reignite your motivation and help you maintain discipline even during challenging times.

Moreover, consider setting new challenges or learning goals that keep you engaged and committed. As an entrepreneur, the landscape is always changing, and there is always something new to learn. By setting developmental goals, you ensure that your commitment to growth remains as strong as your commitment to your business.

In conclusion, long-term discipline isn't just about sticking to a set of rules; it's about developing a lifestyle that inherently supports your continual success and renewal. Habit stacking, understanding the power of the compound effect, and regularly renewing your commitment are not just strategies but essential components of a thriving entrepreneurial life. Each element reinforces the other, creating a robust framework for enduring success and leadership in business.

RECAP AND ACTION ITEMS

Congratulations on diving deep into the art of Mastering Self-Discipline. You've explored the psychological underpinnings of self-control, navigated through common pitfalls, and discovered ways to strengthen your willpower. Moreover, you've equipped yourself with practical strategies to stay on track and grasped the importance of long-term discipline through habit stacking, understanding the compound effect, and ways to renew your commitment.

Now, let's transform this knowledge into action. Here's what you can start doing today to elevate your entrepreneurial journey:

1. Assess Your Current State: Take a moment to reflect on your current self-discipline levels. What are your biggest strengths? Where do you falter? Understanding your starting point will help you measure your progress.

2. Set Clear, Achievable Goals: Utilise the insights from understanding self-discipline to set specific, measurable, and timely goals. Remember, clarity is power.

3. Implement Accountability Systems: Whether it's a digital tool or a personal mentor, establish a system that keeps you accountable. Share your goals with someone you trust to help keep you on track.

4. Experiment with Rewards and Punishments: Tailor this to what motivates you most. Perhaps reward yourself with a weekend getaway after a particularly gruelling project, or set a penalty for missing a deadline.

5. Optimise Your Environment: Remove distractions that hinder your productivity. Whether it's tidying your workspace or using apps that block social media during work hours, make your environment a catalyst for focus.

6. Build and Stack New Habits: Start small. Pick one new habit you want to develop that can lead to greater self-discipline, such as reviewing your day each evening. Once this becomes second nature, add another.

7. Monitor and Adjust Regularly: What gets measured gets managed. Regularly check in on your progress and adjust your strategies as needed. This might mean setting new goals or tweaking your accountability systems.

8. Recommit Often: Self-discipline isn't a one-time effort; it's a continuous process. Set regular intervals, maybe every quarter, to renew your commitment to your discipline goals.

By integrating these steps into your daily and professional life, you'll not only boost your productivity but also lead with greater confidence and control. Remember, the journey to mastering self-discipline is ongoing and evolving. Stay committed, stay disciplined, and watch as you unlock new levels of success in your entrepreneurial ventures.

4

OPTIMISING YOUR WORKSPACE

"Productivity is never an accident. It is always the result of a commitment to excellence, intelligent planning, and focused effort."
— Paul J. Meyer

Physical Space

When you step into your office every morning, what do you feel? Is it a sanctuary where productivity blossoms, or does it feel like a chaotic space where work goes to die? For entrepreneurs and business owners, creating an optimal physical workspace isn't just about aesthetics; it's a fundamental cornerstone of efficiency and success. Let's break down the essentials: ergonomics and comfort, minimising distractions, and crafting the ideal home office.

Ergonomics and Comfort

Starting with the backbone of your workday—quite literally—ergonomics. It's not just a fancy word to throw around during a health and safety meeting; it's about aligning your physical environment to your body's needs, ensuring comfort that lasts throughout marathon sessions of decision-making and innovation.

Consider your chair—your throne in the kingdom of productivity. Is it supporting you like it should? An ergonomic chair does more than just feel comfortable; it adjusts to support your spine's natural curvature, has adjustable armrests and seat height, and provides adequate lumbar support. Remember, discomfort is a distraction you can't afford.

Your desk, be it standing or traditional, plays a pivotal role too. A standing desk can be a game changer, reducing the risks associated with prolonged sitting such as back pain and lethargy. If you prefer a traditional desk, ensure it's at a height where your eyes are level with the top of your computer screen and your arms can comfortably rest parallel to the floor.

Lighting, too, is often overlooked. Poor lighting can strain your eyes and lead to headaches, slashing your productivity. Natural light is ideal, fostering not only visual clarity but also boosting your mood and energy levels. If your workspace lacks natural light, opt for a combination of general and task lighting that mimics natural light as closely as possible.

Minimising Distractions

Distractions in the workspace come in many forms—from the pile of unsorted paperwork glaring at you from your desk to the pings and buzzes of smartphones and emails. Taming these distractions begins with physical organisation.

Start by decluttering. A tidy workspace clears the mind. Invest in storage solutions that keep necessary items within arm's reach but out of immediate sight. This could mean drawer organisers, filing cabinets, or even digital tools that help keep your physical paperwork to a minimum.

Next, consider your digital interruptions. While not strictly part of the 'physical' space, the devices within this space greatly impact your focus. Set boundaries for technology use. This might mean turning off notifications for certain apps, or having 'focus hours' where you only check emails intermittently rather than constantly.

Noise can be another profound distractor, particularly in a home office setting where you might not have the soundproofing luxury of a corporate office. Noise-cancelling headphones can be an excellent investment, or perhaps a white noise machine if you prefer a consistent auditory backdrop.

The Ideal Home Office

Now, let's put it all together in your home office. The goal here is not just to replicate a corporate environment but to enhance it, making it personally optimal for you.

Location is your first decision. Where in your home can you carve out a space that feels separate from your living areas? This psychological separation is crucial for maintaining a work-life balance. A dedicated room is ideal, but if space is a constraint, a designated nook in a quiet part of the house can also serve well.

Personalise your space. This is your command centre, and it should reflect and inspire you. Maybe it's artwork that stimulates creative thinking, or plants that bring a bit of the outdoors inside. The key is to create an environment that energises you and aligns with your work ethos.

Technology is your ally here. Equip your home office with the best tools you can afford—high-speed internet, a powerful computer, and perhaps multiple monitors to expand your digital workspace. These are not just expenses; they are investments in your efficiency and effectiveness.

Finally, consider your access to necessities. Is there a coffee machine nearby for those early starts or late finishes? What about natural light—can you position your desk to take advantage of this free resource? Each element of your home office should contribute to a holistic sense of preparedness and capability.

Optimising your physical workspace is about creating an environment that not only minimises the likelihood of physical strain and distractions but also maximises comfort and personal efficacy. For you, the entrepreneur or business owner, it's about constructing a space where leadership and productivity thrive, where every element conspires to unlock your best self. So take control of your physical space, and watch as it transforms not just your work, but also the trajectory of your business.

Digital Space

Streamlining Digital Tools

In the age where every task seems to demand its own app or software, the digital clutter can quickly become overwhelming. As an entrepreneur, your focus should be on efficiency and effectiveness, not on navigating through a labyrinth of digital tools. Streamlining your digital environment is about choosing the right tools that work together seamlessly, enhancing your productivity rather than hindering it.

Start by auditing your current tech stack. What software are you currently using? What are their purposes? You might find that some of your tools overlap in functionality or that some aren't even being used to their full potential. This is your chance to simplify.

Imagine your digital tools like a well-oiled machine—each part should contribute to the machine's overall effectiveness. For instance, if you're using one tool for email marketing and another for customer relationship management (CRM), check if there is a single platform that integrates both functions. Tools like HubSpot and Salesforce often provide comprehensive solutions that can reduce your switching time between applications.

Moreover, consider the integration capabilities of your chosen tools. Applications that can communicate with each other reduce the need for manual entry and help maintain data consistency. Zapier, for instance, is a great tool for automating workflows between apps that don't naturally communicate with each other.

Lastly, remember to keep this process iterative. As your business grows and evolves, so should your digital toolset. Regularly scheduled reviews of your software needs will ensure that your digital environment remains optimised and clutter-free, allowing you to focus more on growing your business and less on managing it.

Effective Email Management

Email is often seen as one of the biggest productivity killers, yet it remains an essential part of business communication. Managing your inbox effectively is not just about reducing clutter, but also about ensuring that you can extract maximum value from your communications with minimal time expenditure.

One of the first strategies towards effective email management is to adopt the "Inbox Zero" approach. This doesn't mean having zero emails in your inbox all times but rather controlling your inbox so that it doesn't control you. Make it a habit to regularly review, respond, delegate, or delete emails. Tools like SaneBox can be incredibly helpful as they automatically sort incoming emails based on importance, allowing you to focus on what's truly urgent.

Setting up smart filters and labels is another way to keep your inbox organised. Services like Gmail offer robust customisation options that can automatically sort your emails into predefined categories as they arrive. This can help you quickly find emails related to specific projects or from particular contacts.

Furthermore, consider adopting an email schedule. Checking your email continuously throughout the day can fragment your concentration. Instead, allocate specific times for checking your email, such as once in the morning, after lunch, and before you finish your day. This helps in batching your email tasks and keeping your focus on other critical tasks throughout the day.

Lastly, encourage communications that don't necessarily need to be in an email form. Tools like Slack or Microsoft Teams allow for quicker, less formal communication that can often resolve issues more quickly than back-and-forth emails.

Cybersecurity for Entrepreneurs

In today's digital age, cybersecurity is not just a buzzword but a fundamental necessity for protecting your business's sensitive data. As an entrepreneur, understanding and implementing strong cybersecurity measures is crucial, not only to protect your own data but also to safeguard your customers' information.

The first step in fortifying your digital security is to understand the common threats. Phishing attacks, ransomware, and data breaches are among the most prevalent threats that can expose sensitive information to malicious actors. Educating yourself and your team about recognising suspicious emails, links, and requests can significantly reduce the risk of unintentional data leaks.

Implementing robust password policies is another crucial step. Encourage the use of strong, unique passwords for different accounts and implement multi-factor authentication (MFA) wherever possible. Tools like LastPass or 1Password can manage passwords effectively, generating and storing complex passwords that are tough for cybercriminals to crack.

Regularly updating your software is another simple yet effective cybersecurity measure. Software updates often include patches for security vulnerabilities that, if left unaddressed, could be exploited by hackers. Automating these updates can help eliminate the risk of overlooking this critical maintenance task.

Lastly, consider investing in a comprehensive cybersecurity insurance policy. This can provide you with an additional layer of security and peace of mind, knowing that you're financially protected in the event of a cyber attack.

By optimising your digital space through streamlining your tools, managing your email effectively, and securing your online presence, you set a solid foundation for operational excellence. Remember, in the digital realm, efficiency and security don't just support your business—they propel it forward.

Mental Space

Mindfulness at Work

In the relentless hustle of entrepreneurial life, your mental space can often become the most cluttered part of your workspace. Let's kick off with mindfulness, a buzzword that's been bouncing around for a reason. It's about being present, fully engaged with what's happening, what you're doing, and the space you're moving through. That might sound a bit esoteric, especially if you're used to grinding through 14-hour days fuelled by coffee and sheer willpower. But here's the kicker: mindfulness can skyrocket your productivity.

Start your day with a mindfulness exercise - it could be as simple as a five-minute meditation using an app on your smartphone. The goal here is to clear the mental clutter and prepare your brain for the day ahead. This isn't about emptying your mind; rather, it's about focusing it. Think about it like tuning an instrument before a concert or warming up before a sprint. You're setting the stage for optimum performance.

Throughout the day, take 'mindful moments'—short breaks where you step back from the business chaos and recalibrate. It could be a minute of deep breathing, a quick stroll around your office, or even standing by your desk and stretching. These moments can prevent burnout and maintain your mental clarity, keeping your decision-making sharp and your creativity flowing.

Cognitive Load Management

Next up, cognitive load management, a fancy term for managing how much your brain is juggling at any given moment. As an entrepreneur, you're often forced to wear multiple hats - CEO, marketing expert, salesperson, customer service, and sometimes even the IT guy. However, multitasking, as you might glorify it, can be a productivity killer.

The science is clear: our brains aren't designed to handle constant task-switching. Each switch might waste only a fraction of a second, but it adds up, and it exhausts your mental energy much faster than if you maintain a singular focus. So, prioritisation becomes your best friend. Identify the tasks that will have the most significant impact and delegate or defer the rest. Tools like the Eisenhower Box can be incredibly effective here; it helps you decide on and prioritise tasks by urgency and importance, not just the noise they make in your head.

Technology can both be a boon and a bane. Leverage it to manage your cognitive load by automating routine tasks. Whether it's scheduling social media posts or managing customer enquiries, there's likely a tool that can take some weight off your shoulders. Automation frees up space in your brain for more critical thinking and decision-making.

Emotional Intelligence in Business

Lastly, let's talk about emotional intelligence (EI), your ability to understand and manage your emotions and those of others. In the cutthroat world of business, EI is what can set you apart from the competition. It's about more than just playing nice; it's a strategic tool. High EI helps in building resilient teams, forging stronger client relationships, and navigating the high-stakes ups and downs of entrepreneurial life.

Start by developing self-awareness. Monitor your emotional state throughout the day. Recognise what events trigger negative emotions and which ones encourage positive ones. This awareness will allow you to better control your reactions and improve your decision-making process under stress.

Empathy is another critical component of EI. This doesn't just mean sympathising with others; it's about truly understanding their perspectives and needs, which can significantly enhance your leadership and negotiation skills. For instance, understanding a client's underlying concerns can help you address their needs more effectively, often leading to better business outcomes.

Lastly, EI involves managing relationships. This means not only being aware of your own emotions and those of others but also being able to influence and inspire people. As a leader, your ability to maintain morale and motivate your team is crucial. Regular feedback, open communication, and recognising your team's efforts can foster a positive work environment and lead to greater productivity.

By optimising your mental space through mindfulness, effective cognitive load management, and enhancing your emotional intelligence, you'll not only boost your productivity but also gain a deeper sense of fulfillment from your entrepreneurial journey. Remember, the state of your mental space is as crucial as the physical and digital ones, if not more. By taking control of it, you're setting yourself up for not just surviving in this competitive business world, but thriving.

RECAP AND ACTION ITEMS

You've just equipped yourself with some invaluable strategies to optimise your workspace for maximum productivity. From refining your physical environment to enhancing your digital workflows and nurturing your mental space, each adjustment is a step towards a more efficient, focused, and resilient you.

Let's quickly summarise the key takeaways and outline practical action steps you can implement right away.

Physical Space: Remember, comfort and ergonomics are not just about preventing discomfort; they are essential for long-term productivity. Start by adjusting your chair, desk, and computer setup to promote good posture. Next, eliminate distractions in your immediate environment. This could mean investing in noise-cancelling headphones or setting clear boundaries for work interruptions. Finally, create an ideal home office that reflects your personal style and enhances your ability to focus—consider the lighting, colours, and personal items that motivate you.

Action Steps:

1. Assess your current workspace for ergonomic correctness

2. Identify three main distractions and devise a plan to minimise them

3. Personalise your workspace with elements that boost your mood and productivity.

Digital Space:

Streamlining your digital tools can drastically cut down on time wasted navigating clutter. Consolidate apps and software that serve similar functions and unsubscribe from unnecessary services. For email management, adopt a system for checking and organising emails at set times of the day to avoid constant interruptions. Lastly, protect your digital assets with robust cybersecurity measures — a necessity that can't be overlooked in today's digital age.

Action Steps:

1. List all digital tools you currently use and eliminate redundancies

2. Create an email schedule and stick to it, using tools like filters and folders to stay organised

3. Enhance your cybersecurity with updated software, strong passwords, and regular data backups.

Mental Space:

Cultivating a strong mental space is paramount. Practice mindfulness to stay present and reduce stress during your workday. Manage your cognitive load by breaking tasks into smaller, manageable parts and using techniques like the Pomodoro Technique to maintain focus. Develop your emotional intelligence by being mindful of your reactions and understanding the emotions of those around you, which can lead to better business outcomes.

Action Steps:

1. Incorporate a 10-minute mindfulness practice into your daily routine

2. Apply the Pomodoro Technique to at least one of your daily tasks

3. Reflect daily on emotional responses and interactions, seeking continuous improvement.

By transforming your workspace across these three dimensions, you'll not just enjoy immediate gains in productivity, but also cultivate a sustainable environment that fosters long-term business growth and personal well-being. Remember, the ultimate workspace isn't built overnight. It's a continual process of refinement and adjustment. So, get started today, and keep tweaking as you discover what works best for you. Let's unlock your productivity potential!

5

LEVERAGING TECHNOLOGY FOR PRODUCTIVITY

"The best way to predict the future is to invent it." - Alan Kay

Essential Tech Tools

In the fast-paced world of entrepreneurship, leveraging the right technology can make the difference between leading the pack and lagging behind. Let's dive into some essential tech tools that can streamline your operations, boost your productivity, and ensure you stay on top of your game.

Task Management Software

In the tumult of daily business operations, it's easy to get bogged down by a barrage of tasks. This is where task management software comes into its own, acting as your digital personal assistant. Think of it as a tool that doesn't just remind you of what needs to be done but helps prioritise and manage your tasks efficiently.

For instance, tools like Asana and Trello allow you to create projects, assign tasks, set deadlines, and update statuses. The beauty of these platforms lies in their flexibility and accessibility. Whether you're at your desk or on the move, you can keep tabs on your team's progress and adjust on the fly. This is not just about keeping a checklist; it's about creating a workflow that allows you and your team to operate in a synchronised manner, reducing the time wasted on unnecessary meetings and follow-ups.

Moreover, integrating these tools with other applications you use can enhance their functionality. Imagine having your task management software synced with your calendar, email, and even direct messaging systems. This level of integration means you're always informed and prepared for what's next, without having to juggle multiple apps.

Automated Scheduling

Time, as they say, is money, especially for entrepreneurs. Automated scheduling tools are like having an incredibly efficient PA who takes care of all the back-and-forth typically involved in setting up meetings. Tools such as Calendly or Doodle simplify this process by allowing others to see your available slots and book appointments directly, which syncs instantly with your calendar.

This technology shines in its ability to cut down the tedious email chains that often precede meetings. It avoids the confusion of time zone conversions and the error-prone process of manual scheduling. What's more, these tools often come with customizable features like buffer times between appointments, setting maximum numbers of meetings per day, and even integrating with other tools such as Zoom or Skype for setting up virtual meetings seamlessly.

For you, the impact is immediate. Less time spent organising your day means more time spent making strategic decisions and driving your business forward. Furthermore, it sends a message to clients and colleagues alike that you value your time—and theirs. This not only increases efficiency but also enhances your professional image.

Mobile Productivity Apps

In an era where business happens on the go, mobile productivity apps have become indispensable. These apps ensure that being out of the office doesn't mean being out of the loop. Whether it's editing documents on the fly, accessing customer data while in transit, or managing your expenses single-handedly, these tools empower you to operate from anywhere.

Apps like Evernote for note-taking, Google Drive for file management, and QuickBooks for on-the-go accounting are just the tip of the iceberg. Each app addresses specific aspects of business management, ensuring that no matter where you are, your business runs smoothly.

The key advantage here is accessibility. With cloud-based technology, the days of being tied to a desktop are long gone. You can pull up any document, attend any meeting, or send out invoices straight from your smartphone or tablet. This flexibility not only boosts your productivity but also helps maintain a healthy work-life balance, as you're no longer required to be at the office to get things done.

Moreover, the security features integrated into these apps mean that your data is protected, even when accessed over public Wi-Fi networks. With regular updates and patches, mobile productivity apps not only keep your data secure but also ensure that the tools evolve as your business grows.

Incorporating these essential tech tools into your business isn't just about keeping up with the times; it's about setting yourself up for success. Task management software keeps your projects on track, automated scheduling frees up valuable time, and mobile productivity apps let you manage your business from anywhere in the world. Together, these tools don't just help manage your workload—they enhance your capacity to lead and innovate. By integrating these technologies into your daily operations, you're not just surviving in the entrepreneurial world; you're thriving.

Harnessing the Power of AI

AI for Business Analytics

Imagine you could peek into the future and see how your business decisions pan out. Well, while we're not quite at the stage of crystal balls, AI in business analytics is about as close as you can get. It allows you to not just collect data, but to understand and utilise it, predicting trends and outcomes with a precision that was previously the stuff of fiction.

For you, the savvy entrepreneur, leveraging AI in your analytics means you can make faster, more informed decisions. Think of it like having a supercharged assistant who doesn't sleep; constantly analysing market conditions, consumer behaviour, and financial fluctuations. Tools like IBM's Watson or Google's AI offer platforms where massive datasets are no longer monstrous but manageable, and more importantly, actionable.

The key here is integration. Your business probably uses tools like CRM systems, financial software, and various operational tech. AI excels in pulling these threads together, offering insights that are not only based on historical data but also predictive in nature. For instance, AI can help anticipate market demands, allowing you to adjust your inventory or service offerings before your competitors even sense a change.

Moreover, AI-driven analytics can flag areas of waste or inefficiency that are eating into your margins. Perhaps it's identifying a supply chain bottleneck or a poorly performing ad campaign. By addressing these issues proactively, you're not just saving money; you're enhancing your operational agility.

Automated Customer Service

Now, let's talk about your customers. They're the kings and queens of your business realm, right? Automated customer service via AI isn't just about cutting costs by reducing the number of customer service reps you need; it's about enhancing the quality of service they receive.

Chatbots and virtual assistants, powered by AI, are now capable of handling a wide array of customer interactions—from answering frequently asked questions to managing returns and exchanges. Platforms like Zendesk or Drift integrate these AI tools seamlessly into your existing customer service framework, providing a 24/7 service that waits on no man.

The beauty of AI in this space is its learning capability. Initially, AI can handle straightforward queries, but as it learns from interactions, its ability to resolve more complex issues enhances. This not only improves efficiency but also customer satisfaction—your clients are getting quick, accurate responses, and only the most complex issues need to be escalated to human operatives.

Moreover, AI can analyse customer interaction data to identify trends and pain points. Perhaps there are recurring complaints about a particular product feature, or maybe an instruction manual isn't as clear as it could be. By quickly identifying and addressing these issues, you not only solve individual problems but also enhance your product and service offerings.

AI-driven Market Research

Last but certainly not least, let's dive into how AI can transform your approach to market research. Traditional market research can be like trying to find a needle in a haystack. It's often time-consuming and costly. AI simplifies this by not only accelerating data collection but also by enhancing the precision of insights gathered.

Tools like Crayon or MarketMuse use AI to track competitor activity across a myriad of channels, providing you with real-time insights into their strategies, pricing adjustments, and customer feedback. This kind of intel is gold dust; it allows you to stay one step ahead, adapting your strategies in real-time rather than reacting when it's too late.

Furthermore, AI tools analyse social media trends and online consumer behaviour, giving you a bird's-eye view of what's hot and what's not. This isn't just about jumping on every trend but understanding how these trends can be leveraged to attract new customers or develop new products.

The real power of AI-driven market research lies in its predictive capabilities. By analysing current trends and historical data, AI can help predict where the market is headed. This means you can start developing products or adjusting your marketing strategies to meet future demand, positioning you as a leader, not a follower, in your industry.

In harnessing the power of AI across these three areas—business analytics, customer service, and market research—you're not just keeping up with the times; you're setting the pace. The key is to start small if you need to, integrate AI into one area, and as you see the tangible benefits it brings, expand its use across other parts of your business. The future isn't just coming; it's already here, and AI is very much leading the charge.

Staying Ahead of Tech Trends

In the fast-evolving world of technology, staying updated isn't just an advantage; it's a necessity, especially for you as an entrepreneur aiming to keep your business at the peak of productivity and innovation. Here's how you can keep your finger on the pulse of technological advancements and ensure that your business does not just keep up but stays ahead.

Continuous Learning

In an age where information is as accessible as it is abundant, continuous learning emerges as a cornerstone for personal and professional growth. As a business owner, fostering a culture of education and adaptability within your company can lead to significant competitive advantages.

Begin by setting a personal example. Dedicate time each week to educate yourself about new technologies relevant to your industry. Whether it's through online courses, webinars, or specialised podcasts, make learning an integral part of your routine. Platforms like Coursera, Udemy, and LinkedIn Learning offer a plethora of courses tailored to everything from blockchain basics to advanced machine learning.

Encouraging your team to engage in learning is equally important. Consider implementing a learning management system (LMS) that allows employees to take courses during work hours. Some businesses offer incentives for completing courses, such as certificates, bonuses, or even career advancement opportunities. This not only enhances their skills but also boosts morale and retention.

Moreover, attending tech conferences, either virtually or in person, can be a game-changer. These events are not just about passive listening but are interactive opportunities to engage with innovators and thought leaders. You can gain insights into emerging technologies long before they hit the mainstream market, giving you a strategic edge in applying them to your business operations.

Networking in Tech Circles

Building a robust network within tech circles can provide you with a reservoir of knowledge and resources that can be pivotal in navigating the tech landscape. Start by identifying key influencers, thought leaders, and practitioners within your industry and beyond. Social media platforms like LinkedIn and Twitter are excellent for this purpose, offering direct access to the minds shaping the future of technology.

Engaging with these networks goes beyond just connecting online. Participate actively in discussions, share your insights, and ask questions. This engagement can elevate your understanding of tech trends and introduce you to tools and techniques that could revolutionise your business processes.

Moreover, consider joining specialised tech groups or forums online. Platforms such as Stack Exchange, or industry-specific groups on Facebook and LinkedIn, host a vibrant community of tech enthusiasts from whom you can learn a great deal. These communities are often the first to discuss and dissect the latest tech tools and trends, giving you a front-row seat to the future.

Local tech meetups and workshops can also be incredibly beneficial. These gatherings provide a more personal way to build relationships with other tech-savvy entrepreneurs and developers. Such interactions can lead to collaborations, partnerships, or even just valuable advice that could help in making more informed decisions about integrating technology into your business.

Strategic Technology Investments

Investing in technology strategically can significantly enhance your business's productivity and efficiency. However, the key lies in discerning which technologies align with your business goals and can deliver the best return on investment.

Start by conducting a thorough audit of your current technology stack. Identify gaps where new tech could streamline operations or where existing tools are underutilised. This audit should involve input from various departments within your company to ensure all potential tech benefits are captured.

Once you've pinpointed areas for improvement, research technologies that fill these gaps. This could range from adopting more comprehensive CRM systems, integrating IoT devices to enhance your product offerings, or utilising AI-driven analytics for better decision-making. However, the trick isn't just to adopt new technology but to integrate it seamlessly with your existing processes. This might require additional training for your team or hiring specialists who can manage these new systems effectively.

Finally, keep an eye on the ROI of any tech investment. This doesn't just include the financial return but also improvements in customer satisfaction, employee productivity, and brand reputation. Regularly review the impact of these technologies and be prepared to pivot or upgrade as better options become available.

In conclusion, staying ahead in the tech game isn't just about adopting the latest gadgets or software. It's about cultivating a mindset of continuous learning, actively engaging with the tech community, and making strategic investments that align with your long-term business objectives. By taking these steps, you ensure that your business not only keeps pace with technological advancements but uses them to drive growth and innovation.

RECAP AND ACTION ITEMS

Congratulations on completing this deep dive into leveraging technology for enhanced productivity. You've explored a vast array of tools and strategies designed to revolutionise your workday and business operations. Let's ensure that you can implement this knowledge for maximum benefit.

1. Integrate Essential Tech Tools: Start by auditing your current tools and identify any gaps where the essential tech tools discussed could enhance efficiency. Implement task management software to keep your projects on track, set up automated scheduling to save time, and leverage mobile productivity apps to keep you efficient on the move. Remember, the goal is to streamline your operations so you can focus more on growth and less on administrative tasks.

2. Harness the Power of AI: Artificial Intelligence is reshaping how businesses operate. If you haven't already, begin by integrating AI to analyse your business data. This could provide insights you've never considered, driving decisions that push you ahead of the competition. Also, consider AI-driven tools for customer service to enhance customer satisfaction and for market research to identify new business opportunities quickly and accurately.

3. Stay Ahead of Tech Trends: In the fast-evolving tech landscape, continuous learning is your greatest tool. Dedicate time each week to educate yourself about new technologies and their applications in business. Network with tech experts and peers to exchange valuable insights and experiences. Evaluate and invest in emerging technologies that align with your business vision and can provide a competitive edge.

By systematically applying these strategies, you're not just keeping up; you're staying ahead. Transform these insights into action and watch as your business grows, not just efficiently but also more dynamically. Remember, in the world of technology, being proactive rather than reactive is the key to success. Embrace these technologies, and lead your business fearlessly into a productive future.

6

BUILDING AND LEADING PRODUCTIVE TEAMS

"Coming together is a beginning. Keeping together is progress. Working together is success." – Henry Ford

Recruitment Strategies

When you're at the helm of a business, crafting a team that meshes well and galvanises your company's growth is no trivial feat. It's a nuanced art, blending skill, intuition, and strategy. Let's dive into the pivotal aspects of recruitment strategies that can make or break the productivity of your team.

Hiring for Cultural Fit

First things first, let's talk about cultural fit. It's a term that buzzes through the corporate world, often misunderstood as hiring people who simply gel with you on a personal level. But here's the real scoop: hiring for cultural fit means more than finding someone you'd enjoy a pint with. It's about aligning core values, work ethics, and long-term visions between the candidate and your company.

Imagine this: you run a startup that's all about agile, innovative approaches to problems. Hiring someone who's technically adept but prefers a structured, unchanging environment is like trying to fit a square peg in a round hole. Sooner or later, friction arises.

To get this right, you need to define what your company's culture embodies. Are you all about innovation, transparency, and flexibility? Or does your company thrive on structure, hierarchy, and routine? Once you have this nailed down, weave these elements into your job descriptions, interviews, and even the platforms where you post your job listings.

During interviews, ask questions that unearth a candidate's real values and work style. For instance, questions like "Can you describe an environment in which you feel you wouldn't thrive?" or "How do you handle change and ambiguity in the workplace?" can reveal much about their suitability in your cultural landscape.

The Importance of Diversity

Moving on, diversity isn't just a buzzword to splash across your company's CSR page. It's a robust strategy for skyrocketing your company's creativity, problem-solving capabilities and, yes, productivity. Diverse teams bring varied perspectives to the table, crafting innovative solutions that might elude a more homogenous group.

But here's a kicker: diversity goes beyond ticking boxes on ethnicity, gender, or age. It encompasses diversity of thought, experiences, and backgrounds. When you bring people together from varied life paths, you've got yourself a melting pot of ideas that can challenge conventional thinking and lead to breakthroughs in how your business tackles challenges.

How do you recruit for diversity? Start by broadening your recruitment channels. Don't just stick to the usual suspects; explore niche job boards, work with community groups, and tap into professional networks that advocate for underrepresented groups.

In your job ads and interviews, steer clear of jargon and criteria that could unwittingly alienate potential candidates. Be explicit about your commitment to diversity and frame your job descriptions to appeal to a broad audience. During interviews, ensure your questions are structured and consistent across all candidates to avoid unconscious biases influencing your decision.

Skills Versus Potential

Now, let's hash out a debate as old as time in the recruitment world: skills versus potential. On one side of the ring, you have clear, demonstrable skills. On the other, the tantalising possibility of what a person could achieve. Spoiler alert: there's no one-size-fits-all answer here. But, as a business leader, leaning too heavily on one side could mean missing out on some stellar talent.

Hiring for skills makes sense in roles where technical expertise is non-negotiable. Think of roles in IT, law, or medicine, where specific knowledge and competencies are mandatory from day one. But even here, don't overlook the candidate's capacity to learn and grow. Industries evolve, and so should your team.

On the flip side, potential is your golden ticket in fast-evolving environments where adaptability and learning are part of the daily grind. When you hire for potential, you're looking at traits like curiosity, drive, and the ability to mesh with your team's dynamics and grow into roles.

To balance skills and potential, start with a clear picture of what success looks like for the role. If it's heavily skewed towards immediate, specific outputs, prioritise skills but don't neglect attitude and soft skills. For roles that evolve or contribute to long-term strategy, weigh potential more heavily. During interviews, probe into how candidates have adapted to past roles, solved unexpected challenges, or learned new skills. This can give you a glimpse into their potential to rise and evolve with your company.

As you navigate through these waters of recruitment, remember, assembling a productive team is less about finding stars in isolation and more about creating constellations that shine together. Each of these strategies—hiring for cultural fit, fostering diversity, and balancing skills with potential—are threads in the same tapestry, each crucial to the strength and vibrancy of the final picture.

Effective Communication

In the world of business, where every second counts, mastering the art of effective communication within your team isn't just important—it's essential. Let's dive into how you can streamline your communication channels, enhance feedback mechanisms, and manage your remote teams effectively.

Tools for Team Communication

First off, choosing the right tools is the bedrock of flawless team communication. In today's digital age, there's no shortage of platforms designed to keep your team connected, but the key is to select tools that best fit your team's needs and the nature of your projects.

Consider Slack or Microsoft Teams for instant messaging and quick updates. These platforms allow you to create different channels for various projects or departments, helping keep conversations organised and focused. For video conferencing, Zoom and Google Meet are reliable staples that facilitate face-to-face interaction regardless of where team members are located.

Don't overlook the power of project management tools like Asana, Trello, or

Monday.com. These are fantastic for tracking tasks, deadlines, and progress, which keeps everyone in the loop and moving in sync. The visual aspect of these tools also helps in quickly assessing project status at a glance, which is crucial for fast-paced environments.

However, the magic happens when these tools are not just implemented, but optimally integrated into daily workflows. Regular training sessions can help ensure everyone is proficient and comfortable with these tools, thus maximising their potential to enhance your team's communication.

Feedback Mechanisms

Next, let's talk about establishing robust feedback mechanisms. Feedback is the cornerstone of improvement and innovation, and setting up an effective system for it ensures that your team not only stays on track but also feels valued and understood.

One practical approach is the 'Start, Stop, Continue' method. Regularly ask your team members what they believe should be started, stopped, and continued. This can be done via anonymous surveys or during open forum meetings where everyone feels safe to express their thoughts without fear of repercussions.

Another effective technique is the implementation of 360-degree feedback. This method allows team members to receive feedback from their peers, subordinates, and superiors, providing a well-rounded view of their performance. It can highlight different perspectives and areas for improvement that might not be visible from a single viewpoint.

Remember, the goal of feedback isn't to criticise but to help each other grow. Therefore, it's crucial that feedback is always given constructively and accompanied by specific examples. Regular feedback sessions, coupled with real-time recognition of accomplishments, can significantly boost morale and productivity.

Managing Remote Teams

Finally, managing remote teams—a reality for many entrepreneurs today. The key here is not just about utilising technology but also about building a culture that supports remote work.

Firstly, establish clear expectations. When your team knows exactly what is expected of them, including deliverables and deadlines, it eliminates ambiguity and fosters accountability. Make sure these expectations are communicated clearly and reiterated often.

Secondly, trust is crucial. Remote work often eliminates the possibility of spontaneous desk chats that you would have in an office setting. Hence, it's important to trust your team to manage their time and tasks effectively. This trust can be built through regular check-ins rather than constant monitoring, which can come off as micromanaging.

Encourage a healthy work-life balance by respecting off-hours and fostering an environment where it's okay to step away from the desk. Use tools like Slack's 'Do Not Disturb' feature to allow team members to carve out focus time without interruptions.

Lastly, make time for team bonding. Remote teams miss out on the casual coffee breaks that naturally occur in an office setting. Organise virtual coffee breaks or after-work hangouts to help build rapport and maintain a team spirit. These informal gatherings can be pivotal in building strong, cooperative teams.

By embracing these strategies, you can ensure that your team communicates effectively, regardless of whether they're down the hall or across the globe. Remember, in the realm of business, clear and effective communication isn't just about sharing information—it's about fostering understanding, building trust, and driving your team towards shared goals.

Inspiring Leadership

Leading by Example

In the realm of business, actions speak louder than words. As a leader, the way you behave sets the tone for your team's conduct and ultimately shapes the culture of your organisation. It's about showing, not just telling. If you're committed to punctuality, diligence, and integrity, these traits need to be evident in your daily operations, not just bullet points in a company handbook.

Consider the impact of a leader arriving on time, prepared, and ready to engage. It communicates respect and sets an expectation of professionalism that is contagious. Similarly, by openly engaging with challenges and maintaining composure under pressure, you model resilience and problem-solving in real-time, providing your team with a clear example of how to handle crises.

Moreover, transparency about your own development areas can foster an environment where continuous learning and honesty are valued. Share your journey towards improving certain skills or knowledge areas. This not only humanises you but also encourages your team to pursue their growth without fear of judgment.

Empowering Team Members

Empowerment is a buzzword in many leadership discussions, but it's truly a fundamental element in unlocking the potential of your team. To empower is to provide your team with the authority, resources, and confidence to take initiative and make decisions. This doesn't mean leaving them to sink or swim; rather, it's about guiding them to become leaders in their own right.

Start by delegating meaningful tasks that stretch their capabilities. It's crucial, however, to ensure that these tasks are accompanied by clear objectives and the necessary resources to achieve them. This approach not only enhances their skills but also builds trust—a critical currency in any business.

Feedback plays a pivotal role here. Regular, constructive feedback helps team members understand their progress and areas for improvement. But empowerment also involves listening. Encourage your team to voice their ideas and solutions. When they know their input genuinely influences outcomes, engagement and innovation flourish.

Finally, consider creating leadership opportunities within projects or committees. These platforms allow team members to experience leadership roles in a supportive setting, preparing them for more substantial roles in the future.

Creating a Vision

Vision is the art of seeing what is invisible to others. As a leader, one of your key roles is to craft and communicate a compelling vision—a clear, inspiring picture of the future that your team can rally behind. This vision should not only reflect where the company is headed but also resonate on a personal level with each member of your team.

Crafting this vision requires deep reflection on the values and goals that define your business. What makes your company unique? What impact do you aim to have on your customers and the broader community? Once defined, this vision needs to be woven into every communication and strategy meeting. It should be the backdrop against which all decisions are made, providing a consistent reminder of what you all are working towards.

But creating a vision is only half the battle. The next step is to ensure it is shared and embraced by your team. This involves clear and frequent communication, using stories and examples to paint a vivid picture of the desired future. It's also helpful to link the vision to your team's daily tasks and goals, showing how their efforts contribute to the larger picture.

Moreover, celebrate milestones that align with the vision. These celebrations reinforce the significance of the vision and motivate the team to continue pushing towards it. Whether it's a small win or a major breakthrough, taking the time to recognise and reward these moments can have a profound effect on team morale and cohesion.

Inspiring leadership is about more than just driving productivity; it's about creating an environment where people feel valued, visions are shared, and potentials are reached. By leading by example, empowering your team, and crafting a compelling vision, you set the stage for sustainable success and a culture that thrives on innovation and commitment. Remember, the strength of your leadership is measured not by your power to push but by your ability to pull others towards greatness.

RECAP AND ACTION ITEMS

Congratulations! You've just armed yourself with a powerhouse of strategies to build and lead a highly productive team. Let's quickly recap the essentials and then dive into some practical steps you can take right away.

In the realm of recruitment, remember that hiring isn't just about filling a vacancy but about finding a true fit for your company culture. Embrace diversity not as a checkbox but as a strategy to inject various perspectives and innovation into your team. Always weigh skills against potential; sometimes a less experienced candidate could bring exponential growth and fresh energy to your team.

Moving on to communication—this is the glue that holds your team together. Implementing effective tools and establishing robust feedback mechanisms are crucial. Whether your team works from an office or remotely, fostering a culture of clear and consistent communication will prevent misunderstandings and build a strong, unified group.

Leadership is where your personal influence comes into play. Lead by example—your team will follow suit if they see you embodying the values you preach. Empower them by delegating meaningful tasks and showing trust in their capabilities. Lastly, continually craft and refine your vision, sharing it compellingly to guide your team towards common goals.

ACTION STEPS:

1. Review your current hiring processes: Are you looking beyond the resume? Consider setting up a system that evaluates cultural fit and potential, not just skills.

2. Diversify your recruitment channels: This could involve reaching out to different networks or communities that you haven't tapped into before.

3. Evaluate your communication tools: Are they up to date and effective? Perhaps introduce a new tool that better meets the needs of your evolving team, especially if managing remote workers.

4. Set up a regular feedback schedule: This could be weekly, bi-weekly, or monthly, but keep it consistent. Use it as a two-way street where you can offer guidance and they can voice concerns or suggestions.

5. Reflect on your leadership style: Are there areas where you could be more of a role model? Pick one aspect to improve on, be it transparency, accountability, or supportiveness.

6. Delegate a significant project: Show trust and empower your team by handing over the reins on a project you would typically handle yourself.

7. Revisit and communicate your business vision: Ensure it aligns with your current operations and future ambitions. Share this vision in your next team meeting to re-energise and refocus efforts.

By taking these steps, you'll not only boost your team's productivity but also foster an environment where creativity and efficiency thrive. Remember, the strength of a leader is measured by the success of their team. Equip yourself to be that formidable leader who not only expects excellence but also provides the tools and support to achieve it.

7

MASTERING TIME-BLOCKING AND DELEGATION

"The key is not to prioritise what's on your schedule, but to schedule your priorities." - Stephen Covey

Principles of Time-Blocking

The Basics of Time-Blocking

Time-blocking is a potent method to take command of your day, rather like a chess master strategically moving pieces across the board. At its core, it involves dividing your day into blocks of time, each dedicated to a specific task or group of tasks. This method not only helps in prioritising what needs to be done but also when and how long it should take.

Start by visualising your typical workday. You probably have about eight to ten hours that can be carved up for various tasks. The key is not to allow the day to dictate what you do, but for you to dictate the day. For instance, you might block off an hour in the morning for emails, follow it with a two-hour block for deep work like brainstorming new business strategies, then perhaps a block for meetings, and so on.

The beauty of time-blocking is that it operates on the principle of constrained time; you allocate a specific amount of time for an activity and that's all the time you get. It forces efficiency because you know there's a hard stop. It also minimises the risk of tasks bleeding into each other, which can often lead to workday sprawl — that feeling when the day seems to stretch endlessly and yet, frustratingly, little gets accomplished.

Common Challenges

While the system sounds simple, its implementation often meets with a few common hurdles. Distraction is the prime adversary. In an age where notifications can constantly interrupt, maintaining focus within your time blocks can feel like a Herculean task. To combat this, consider leveraging technology to your advantage: use apps that block distracting websites or notifications during your focused work blocks.

Another challenge is underestimating the amount of time tasks might take, leading to either overflow or unfinished tasks. This is where the art of estimation and adjustment comes into play. Initially, your estimates might be off, but as you continue with time-blocking, you'll get better at gauging how much time different tasks require. Remember, flexibility isn't the enemy of structure. Adjust your blocks as necessary, but keep the discipline of sticking to them as closely as possible.

Lastly, there's the psychological hurdle. The rigidity of time-blocking can sometimes feel stifling. It's important to integrate breaks and buffer times between blocks to give your brain a rest. Just as a muscle grows during rest periods, your cognitive abilities recharge when you step back momentarily.

Advanced Time-Blocking Strategies

Once you've mastered the basics and navigated through the common challenges, you're ready to elevate your time-blocking strategy. One advanced technique is to theme your days. For example, Monday could be your administrative day for handling all back-office tasks, while Tuesday could be client-focused. This method not only streamlines thinking but also sets clear expectations for what each day entails, reducing decision fatigue.

Another strategy is to leverage your natural energy fluctuations throughout the day. If you're a morning person, block your most demanding tasks in the morning when your energy and concentration are at their peak. Save the lower-energy tasks for the afternoon slump.

Moreover, consider integrating what's known as 'buffer blocks' — short periods set aside to deal with overflow tasks or unexpected demands that arise. These act as a pressure release valve to ensure that when interruptions happen, they don't throw off your entire schedule.

Lastly, make strategic use of 'review blocks' at the end of the week. This is a time to assess what's working and what isn't. Did some tasks consistently overrun their time blocks? Are there blocks that consistently end early? Use this insight to tweak your blocks for the following week, ensuring continuous improvement and adaptation in your approach.

Time-blocking isn't just a scheduling technique; it's a philosophy of deliberate focus. It's about making time for what truly moves the needle in your business and ensuring that you're not just busy, but productive. By mastering this method, you set yourself up not just to work smarter, but to lead more effectively, ensuring your business thrives in the ever-competitive market.

The Art of Delegation

When to Delegate

In the life of any business owner, there comes a pivotal moment when you realise you simply can't do everything yourself. Recognising when to delegate is crucial not just for your productivity but also for your mental well-being and the growth of your business.

The first sign that it's time to delegate occurs when you find yourself swamped with tasks that prevent you from focusing on the core activities that only you can perform. These activities are typically tied directly to the growth and strategic direction of your business. If you're spending a significant portion of your day on administrative tasks, customer support, or any other operational activities that don't require your unique expertise, these are prime candidates for delegation.

Another indicator is the feeling of being constantly behind. If deadlines are slipping and you're staying late, it's a sign that the workload is more than one person can handle. Delegating could free up your schedule to focus on high-impact activities that drive the business forward.

Finally, consider delegating when there's someone else who can do a job better than you can. This isn't just about freeing up your time—it's about playing to your team's strengths and achieving better results.

How to Delegate Effectively

Effective delegation is not about offloading tasks you don't enjoy; it's about entrusting tasks to team members in a way that maximises their skills and your time. The following steps can ensure that you delegate effectively:

1. **Choose the Right Tasks to Delegate:** Start with tasks that are time-

consuming and do not necessarily require your level of expertise. Ensure these tasks are well-defined and have clear processes in place.

2. Select the Right Person for the Job: Delegating effectively means matching the task with the person's skills and career aspirations. This not only ensures the job is done well but also helps in developing your team's capabilities.

3. Provide Clear Instructions and Expectations: When delegating, be clear about what success looks like. Provide detailed instructions, deadlines, and the scope of authority they have over the task. Ambiguity can lead to frustration and wasted effort.

4. Set Up a Feedback Loop: Establish a system where you can receive regular updates on progress. This isn't about micromanaging but ensuring the task is on track and providing support where necessary.

5. Empower and Trust Your Team: Delegation involves a certain level of risk, as it can be hard to let go of control. Trust your team by empowering them with the responsibility. This trust is fundamental not only to delegation but to team morale and confidence.

6. Recognise and Reward Effort: Acknowledge the efforts of your team, especially when they achieve desired outcomes. This recognition will foster a positive work environment and encourage further initiative and engagement.

Overcoming Delegation Fears

Delegating can be daunting. Common fears include the belief that no one else can do the task as well as you, the fear of losing control, and the worry that delegation may result in mistakes that reflect poorly on you.

To overcome these fears, start by acknowledging that perfection is an illusion; minor mistakes are part of the learning curve. Focus on the long-term benefits of developing a capable team. Remember, delegation can also be incremental. You don't have to hand over entire projects at once. Start small, delegate minor tasks, and as you gain confidence in your team's abilities, you can delegate more significant responsibilities.

Another way to mitigate these fears is to invest in training. Equip your team with the skills and information they need to succeed. Not only does this prepare them better, but it also builds your confidence in their abilities.

Lastly, maintain an open line of communication. Encourage your team to ask questions and come to you with challenges. This not only ensures that problems are dealt with swiftly but also helps build a culture of openness and continuous improvement.

Delegation is not just a skill but a critical component of leadership. By mastering when and how to delegate, and by overcoming the associated fears, you set your business on a path to greater efficiency and effectiveness. Remember, the goal is not just to make your workload manageable but to enhance team capacity and drive your business's growth.

Tools and Techniques

In the fast-paced world of business, leveraging the right tools can streamline your workflow, amplifying your time-blocking and delegation efforts. Here's a guide to selecting the best apps and software, integrating these tools into your daily routines, and continually evaluating their effectiveness to ensure they meet your evolving business needs.

Best Apps and Software

Navigating the sea of productivity tools can be overwhelming. Yet, the right tools are like a Swiss Army knife for your business, adaptable and resourceful. Whether you're a solopreneur or heading a growing enterprise, some tools have made significant impacts on many successful entrepreneurs' lives.

For time-blocking, **Calendly** and **Google Calendar** stand out due to their user-friendly interfaces and robust integration capabilities. Calendly helps in scheduling meetings without the back-and-forth emails, integrating seamlessly with your Google Calendar to show your availability and allowing others to book slots accordingly. Google Calendar can be used for colour-coding different types of activities, giving you a clear visual of your day at a glance.

When it comes to delegation, tools like **Asana** and **Trello** offer intuitive platforms to assign tasks, track progress, and set deadlines. Asana allows for detailed task descriptions and the attachment of necessary documents, facilitating clear communication. Meanwhile, Trello uses a card-based system that is perfect for visual organisers who prefer a board layout to see the progression of projects and tasks.

For communication, **Slack** stands out. It reduces email clutter by allowing for real-time messaging and collaboration. Channels can be set up by project, team, or topic, ensuring information is organised and accessible.

Lastly, if you're looking for an all-encompassing tool, **Monday.com** offers a flexible platform that combines elements of project management, time-blocking, and effective delegation into one user-friendly interface.

Integrating Tools into Daily Routines

Adopting new tools is only part of the equation. The real magic happens when these tools become integral to your daily routines. Integration requires a strategic approach; it's about making the tools work for you, not the other way around.

Start by defining your workflow. Break your business processes into stages or steps, then match these with functionalities offered by your tools. For instance, if you have a morning routine of planning your day, integrate time-blocking tools directly into this routine by reviewing your digital calendar first thing in the morning and adjusting as necessary. This could also be a good time to review tasks delegated through platforms like Asana or Trello to monitor progress and plan follow-ups.

Automations can significantly enhance this integration. Many productivity tools offer automation features that can handle repetitive tasks. For example, setting up an automation in Slack to send reminders for daily stand-up meetings or integrating your project management tool with your calendar to automatically block time for task deadlines.

Moreover, ensure these tools are accessible across the devices you use throughout the day. Most tools offer mobile versions, which can be incredibly handy for on-the-go adjustments and updates. This way, whether you're at the desk or in the field, your productivity system remains intact.

Evaluating Tool Effectiveness

The business world evolves rapidly, and the effectiveness of tools can shift as your business grows and changes. Regular evaluation of your tools ensures they continue to serve your business needs and provide a return on investment.

Set criteria for evaluation based on what success looks like for your business. This might include metrics like time saved, tasks completed, or reduction in communication mishaps. Use features within the tools to track these metrics. For instance, time-tracking features in project management software can provide insights into time spent on various tasks and projects.

Solicit feedback from your team. They are the primary users and will have valuable insights into what is working and what isn't. This can be done through regular check-ins or setting up a feedback channel on your communication platform.

Additionally, keep an eye on the market for new and updated tools. The perfect tool today might be outpaced by a better solution tomorrow. Subscribe to tech blogs, listen to productivity podcasts, and participate in forums where other entrepreneurs share tool recommendations and hacks.

In conclusion, choosing the right tools, integrating them smoothly into your daily routines, and continually assessing their impact, can dramatically enhance your productivity. By making these tools work seamlessly with your business operations, you not only save time but also create a more structured, efficient, and responsive business environment. Remember, the goal is to make technology work in your favour, freeing you up to focus on strategic decision-making and leadership.

RECAP AND ACTION ITEMS

Congratulations on navigating through the intricacies of time-blocking and delegation! By now, you've armed yourself with the principles needed to carve out blocks of focused time effectively, understood the common pitfalls, and even explored advanced strategies to elevate your efficiency. You've also stepped into the art of delegation, learning not just when and how to delegate, but also how to surmount the psychological barriers that often hinder this essential practice.

Let's transform these insights into tangible results. Here's what you can do next:

1. Start Small with Time-Blocking: Choose one or two tasks this coming week where you will apply strict time-blocking. Observe how these blocks improve your focus and productivity. Remember, the key is consistency, so keep refining your approach based on what works best for your schedule.

2. Evaluate Your Delegation Needs: Make a list of tasks you currently handle that could be delegated. Identify which team member's skills align with these tasks. If you don't have a team member to delegate to, consider if it's time to hire, or perhaps outsource.

3. Implement a Delegation Plan: For each task you've identified, clearly outline the outcome you expect, the resources available, and the deadline. Communicate these to your chosen delegate(s) clearly and set up a follow-up schedule to discuss progress.

4. Choose Your Tools: Reflect on the tools and apps discussed. Select one or two that best fit your business needs and integrate them into your routine. Start with a trial period to assess their impact on your productivity and team dynamics before fully committing.

5. Track and Reflect: Keep a journal or log for at least one month documenting your experiences with time-blocking and delegation. Note any increases in productivity, challenges faced, and how well your tools are supporting your goals.

6. Adjust and Optimise: Based on your reflections, make necessary adjustments. Perhaps a different time-blocking strategy might work better, or a different tool might be more intuitive for your team.

Remember, mastering these skills is not a one-time event but a continuous process of learning and adjusting. Each step you take brings you closer to a more streamlined, efficient, and fearless leadership style. So, keep pushing the boundaries and tweaking your systems until they're just right for you and your enterprise.

With these action steps, you're well on your way to mastering the art of productivity through effective time management and delegation. Keep the momentum going, and watch as your business thrives under your renewed, dynamic leadership.

8

THE ROLE OF CONTINUOUS LEARNING

> "Live as if you were to die tomorrow. Learn as if you were to live forever." - Mahatma Gandhi

Fostering a Learning Mindset

In the fiercely competitive arena of business, where the only constant is change, adopting a learning mindset isn't just an advantage; it's essential for survival and growth. As an entrepreneur, your ability to adapt and grow with your business is what will distinguish you from the rest. This journey begins with fostering a learning mindset, encompassing a growth mindset, learning from failure, and using curiosity as a strategic tool in your business.

The Growth Mindset

The concept of a growth mindset, developed by psychologist Carol Dweck, is profoundly transformative and particularly pertinent for entrepreneurs like you. It revolves around the belief that your basic abilities can be developed through dedication and hard work—brains and talent are just the starting points. This view creates a love of learning and a resilience that is essential for great accomplishment.

Think about the last time you faced a setback in your business. Did you view it as a signal of your limits, or as an opportunity to evolve and enhance your skills? The difference in those perspectives can be the difference between folding under pressure and rising to the occasion.

To cultivate a growth mindset, start by recognising and altering your own beliefs about learning and intelligence. Begin to praise the process, not just the outcomes. When you or your team hit milestones, celebrate the hard work and strategies that got you there, rather than just the success itself. This reinforces the value of persistence and effort, encouraging a continuous journey of improvement.

Moreover, challenge yourself regularly. Stepping out of your comfort zone not only adds to your skill set but also builds resilience. Remember, every master was once a disaster. The more challenges you overcome, the more adept you become at tackling new ones.

Learning from Failure

Failure is an inevitable stepping stone in the journey of business. However, in a learning mindset, failure isn't a badge of disgrace; it's a foundational element for building success. The key, however, lies in your response to these failures.

When a project doesn't turn out as expected, instead of sweeping it under the rug, dissect it. What went wrong? What could be done differently next time? This reflective process transforms failure from a setback into a stepping-stone towards greater understanding and capability.

Consider the stories of numerous successful entrepreneurs and you'll notice a common theme: their biggest breakthroughs often came after significant failures. These are not just tales of persistence, but also of learning. They didn't just try again – they tried smarter.

Creating a culture that doesn't just allow but encourages constructive criticism and openness about failures is crucial. It makes your team stronger and more adaptive. Encourage your staff to share their 'failures' and learning points in regular meetings. Make it clear that every mistake has the potential to lead to greater understanding and improvement.

Curiosity as a Business Strategy

Curiosity might have killed the cat, but it also built some of the most successful businesses in the world. Curiosity leads to innovation. When you're curious, you question how things work and why things are the way they are. You're open to exploring new ideas and discovering new solutions.

Start embedding curiosity into your business strategy by fostering an environment where questioning is encouraged. Make it a habit to question everything from your business processes to your customer service methods. Why do we do it this way? Is there a better, more efficient method? What are we missing? These questions can propel your business to new heights.

Invest in resources that encourage exploration and learning. This could be access to courses, books, or seminars related to your business or industry. Encourage your team to set aside time each week to learn something new, without the pressure of immediate results. This not only upgrades their skills but also refreshes their mindset and sparks innovation.

Moreover, leverage your network. Engage with other business owners and entrepreneurs. Exchanges in such networks can be incredibly enriching, providing fresh perspectives and insights that you might not encounter in your immediate environment.

Incorporating these three facets of a learning mindset into your daily business operations can dramatically transform how you and your team navigate challenges and opportunities. By embracing a growth mindset, learning from failures, and fostering curiosity, you're not just surviving in the business world; you're thriving and leading it forward. As you continue to learn and adapt, remember that each step in this journey not only increases your knowledge but also enhances your capacity to lead fearlessly and efficiently.

Skill Acquisition Techniques

When it comes to scaling the competitive heights of today's business world, mastering new skills is not just an advantage; it's a necessity. The ability to learn rapidly and effectively can dramatically leverage your success, transforming challenges into triumphs. Let's dive into some proven methods you can employ to accelerate your learning curve and enhance your repertoire of skills.

Rapid learning methods

Imagine you could cut the time it takes to master a new skill in half. Sounds enticing, right? Rapid learning techniques, which focus on efficiency and adaptability, can help you do just that. The key here is to embrace a method known as the DiSSS system (Deconstruction, Selection, Sequencing, and Stakes), a concept I find incredibly effective.

First, deconstruct the skill you wish to learn. Break it down into the smallest possible components. For instance, if your goal is to improve your digital marketing skills, you might break this down into components like SEO, content marketing, and social media advertising.

Next, select the most valuable components to learn first. Ask yourself, which of these will give me 80% of the results with 20% of the effort? This is where the Pareto Principle really comes into play. In our digital marketing example, you might choose to focus on mastering SEO first, as it could be the most impactful.

Sequencing is about determining the most effective order to learn the parts you've selected. Sometimes learning things in a logical progression can make a huge difference in how well and how quickly you learn.

Finally, stakes are about creating accountability. Set deadlines for yourself, or even better, make your goals public or create some other form of accountability. This pressure can significantly boost your motivation and commitment.

Learning platforms and resources

In today's digital age, there are myriad resources at your fingertips, designed to make learning new skills not just easier but also more accessible. Choosing the right platforms can make a significant difference in how effectively you absorb new knowledge and apply it to your business.

For interactive learning, platforms like Coursera and Udemy offer courses on a vast array of subjects taught by industry professionals. These platforms often include community discussions that can enhance your learning through engagement with peers.

Moreover, for those who prefer a more hands-on approach, platforms like Codecademy for coding, or HubSpot Academy for marketing, provide practical exercises that are invaluable for skill acquisition in specific fields.

Don't overlook the value of less formal platforms either. Podcasts, YouTube channels, and blogs are fantastic resources for more casual, yet often profoundly insightful learning. For instance, listening to a podcast about behavioural economics could provide you with unexpected ideas to improve your business strategies.

Balancing breadth and depth

As an entrepreneur, you need a broad set of skills to handle the myriad challenges that come your way. However, it's equally important not to spread yourself too thin. The art of balancing breadth and depth in your learning endeavours is crucial.

Start by developing a broad base of essential skills, particularly those that are universally beneficial like leadership, time management, and basic financial literacy. These form the foundation upon which you can build more specific expertise.

Once you have your base, focus on deepening your knowledge in the areas that most directly impact your business outcomes. If you're running a tech startup, for instance, you might want to dive deep into user experience design or agile methodologies.

Remember, going deep doesn't mean getting stuck on perfection. It's about achieving a level of competence that allows you to innovate and execute effectively. Mastery in a specific area can often give you a competitive edge, but the real trick is knowing when you've reached diminishing returns on the time invested.

In conclusion, learning new skills is an ongoing process, essential for any entrepreneur looking to stay relevant and competitive. By employing rapid learning methods, leveraging modern learning platforms, and balancing the breadth and depth of your knowledge, you can significantly enhance your effectiveness as a business leader. Keep these techniques in mind as you continue to push the boundaries of what you and your business can achieve.

Applying Learning to Business Growth

Translating learning into innovation can seem like a nebulous concept, but it's essentially about turning theoretical knowledge into practical, impactful actions. Imagine you've just learned a new method for data analysis. Instead of letting that knowledge sit idle, you apply it to your sales data, uncovering patterns that had been invisible. This could lead you to adjust your marketing strategy, resulting in increased sales and customer engagement. It's about connecting the dots in ways that aren't immediately obvious, which demands a certain boldness—a willingness to experiment and potentially fail.

The true art here lies not in acquiring knowledge, but in applying it creatively and efficiently. Think of it as a kind of alchemy that transforms raw information into the gold of market advantage. This is innovation in its most practical form and it requires an environment where experimentation is encouraged and failures are seen as stepping stones to success.

Moving to case studies of learning-led growth, let's consider a practical example. Take, for instance, a tech startup that pivoted its business model based on behavioural insights gained from user data. Initially focused on a broad, generic software solution, the company used client interactions and feedback to learn about specific pain points. This learning guided them to refine their product into a niche application that addressed those specific issues, significantly boosting their market share and customer satisfaction.

This scenario isn't unique. Many successful companies have thrived by continually adapting and learning. They treat every customer interaction as a learning opportunity, every market change as a lesson to be studied. You, too, can adopt this approach. Analyse your business's case studies—or those of others in your industry—to identify patterns and apply these lessons to your own context.

Lastly, let's delve into continuous improvement models, which are formal strategies to integrate this type of learning and adaptation into the fabric of a business. One widely embraced model is the Lean methodology, which focuses on minimising waste and maximising value. The core idea here is to create more value for customers with fewer resources.

A key component of Lean is the concept of kaizen, or continuous improvement. Kaizen encourages small, incremental changes consistently applied over time, which can lead to substantial improvements. This approach isn't just about efficiency; it's about being committed to constant learning and adaptation.

Implementing a continuous improvement model requires you to establish metrics for success and then regularly review these metrics to identify areas for improvement. It's a cycle of learning, applying, reviewing, and then learning again. This not only helps in refining products and services but also enhances the skills and capabilities of your team, creating a culture of learning and growth.

By integrating these models into your business operations, you ensure that learning and improvement are continuous and that they drive growth. This isn't a one-time project but an ongoing journey that can set you apart from the competition.

Incorporating these elements into your business isn't just about staying competitive. It's about leading the charge in innovation, setting new standards, and continuously finding new ways to deliver value to your customers. Remember, the most successful entrepreneurs are not necessarily those who know the most but those who consistently apply and adapt what they learn to stay ahead of the curve.

RECAP AND ACTION ITEMS

As you've journeyed through the exploration of continuous learning, you've armed yourself with actionable insights to elevate your efficiency, lead fearlessly, and ultimately master your day. Let's briefly recap the critical elements and outline some concrete steps you can take to integrate these learnings into your daily business operations.

You've recognised the importance of fostering a learning mindset, which is pivotal in nurturing your growth mindset, learning from failures, and leveraging curiosity as a strategic tool in business. Embracing these aspects will not only prepare you for the inevitable challenges of entrepreneurship but also fuel your drive for innovation.

In the realm of skill acquisition, you've discovered various rapid learning methods that can accelerate your journey to expertise. You've also explored a slew of learning platforms and resources that are at your disposal, ready to be tapped into. The concept of balancing breadth and depth in learning has underscored the need for a well-rounded yet focused approach to acquiring new skills.

Finally, applying learning to business growth requires a strategic translation of new knowledge into innovative practices. You've seen how other businesses have successfully harnessed continuous learning to propel growth and explored different continuous improvement models that keep a business evolving in a competitive landscape.

Action Steps:

1. **Assess Your Learning Style:** Identify whether you are a visual, auditory, or kinesthetic learner to optimise the absorption of new information. Tailor your learning resources and methods to suit this style.

2. Set Learning Goals: Define clear, measurable learning objectives that align with your broader business goals. Whether it's mastering a new technology or understanding market trends, make sure these goals are specific, achievable, and time-bound.

3. Implement a Learning Schedule: Dedicate specific times in your week for active learning. This could be through reading, taking online courses, or engaging in workshops. Consistency is key.

4. Apply Learning Immediately: Use new knowledge as soon as possible within your business operations to reinforce learning and gauge its effectiveness. This could be through a new marketing strategy or a revamped operational process.

5. Foster a Culture of Learning: Encourage your team to adopt continuous learning by providing them with access to courses, time for learning, and incentives for educational advancements.

6. Review and Iterate: Regularly review the impact of your learning initiatives on business performance. Seek feedback and be ready to make adjustments to your learning strategies to better serve your business goals.

By integrating these steps, you not only evolve as an entrepreneur but also drive your business towards sustained growth and innovation. Remember, the most successful business leaders are those who remain students at heart, perpetually curious and relentlessly pursuing knowledge. Embrace continuous learning as a fundamental business strategy, and you'll unlock levels of productivity and leadership success you never thought possible.

9

BALANCING WORK AND LIFE

> "You will never feel truly satisfied by work until you are satisfied by life." – Heather Schuck

Understanding Work-Life Integration

In the bustling world of entrepreneurship, the quest for a work-life balance can feel like chasing a mythical beast. It's often portrayed as this perfect state where everything aligns seamlessly, but let's be real: the scales are rarely even. This isn't about achieving a mythical 'perfect balance' but rather navigating through the complex interplay of your professional and personal life in a way that works for you. Let's delve deeper into the intricacies of work-life integration, setting practical boundaries, and understanding the broader impacts of achieving a semblance of balance.

The Myth of Perfect Balance

First off, let's bust a common myth: there is no such thing as perfect work-life balance. As an entrepreneur, you might have noticed how your work bleeds into your personal life and vice versa. Trying to maintain an equal balance between work and life every single day is like trying to keep all the plates spinning simultaneously – eventually, one might drop. Instead of striving for perfection, aim for a realistic integration that aligns with your personal values and professional goals.

Think of balance not as a static state but as an ongoing process of prioritisation and negotiation. Some days, your business will demand more attention, and other days, your personal life will need you more. The key is flexibility. By accepting that the scales will tip back and forth, you're better positioned to manage your energy and resources effectively.

Setting Boundaries

One of the most significant steps in mastering work-life integration is setting boundaries. This is crucial, not just for your wellbeing, but also for maintaining the quality of your work and your relationships. Boundaries help you define what you are willing and not willing to tolerate, which in turn helps others understand how to interact with you.

Start by delineating your work hours and sticking to them as much as possible. Communicate these hours clearly to your team, clients, and even family. For instance, you might decide that post7 PM is family time, which means no work calls or emails. It's about making a commitment and respecting your own rules.

Moreover, learn to say no. It's a powerful word that can free up a lot of time and energy. As an entrepreneur, you're likely bombarded with opportunities and requests daily. But not every 'great opportunity' is great for you. Evaluate how each request aligns with your goals and current commitments. If it doesn't fit, have the courage to pass on it.

The Ripple Effects of Work-Life Balance

Achieving a healthier work-life integration has profound ripple effects, influencing various aspects of your life and work. For starters, it can significantly enhance your productivity. When you're not constantly overworked and stretched too thin, you can focus better and produce higher-quality work.

On a personal front, setting boundaries helps prevent burnout. Entrepreneurs often push their limits, but this isn't a sustainable strategy. By integrating downtime and ensuring you recharge, you maintain your health and mental sharpness, which are crucial for long-term success.

Furthermore, a well-integrated work-life approach can improve your relationships. It allows you to be fully present during personal interactions, rather than being distracted by work thoughts. This presence builds stronger connections and can provide emotional support, which every entrepreneur needs given the rollercoaster nature of running a business.

Ultimately, mastering work-life integration isn't just about improving your own quality of life; it's about setting a standard and culture for your business. It reflects in how you handle your team and set expectations. When employees see you prioritising a healthy work-life dynamic, they feel encouraged to do the same, which can lead to lower turnover rates and a happier, more productive team.

As you continue on your entrepreneurial journey, remember that integrating work and life is not about creating a perfect balance but managing an imperfect one with grace and effectiveness. By setting clear boundaries and understanding the impacts of your choices, you can steer your life and business towards a path that not only meets your goals but also preserves your greatest asset: your well-being.

Strategies for Personal Wellbeing

Stress Management Techniques

In the high-stakes game of entrepreneurship, stress is as commonplace as coffee. However, just because it's common doesn't mean it's harmless. Prolonged stress can sap your energy, cloud your judgement, and ultimately, undermine your performance. So, how do you keep these stress gremlins at bay? First, identify your stress triggers. Is it a looming deadline, a difficult client, or perhaps, your inbox that seems more like a black hole? Once you know what flips your stress switch, you can better manage it.

One effective technique is the Pareto Principle, or the 80/20 rule, which can be applied to stress management by identifying the 20% of your sources that are causing 80% of your stress. Focus on resolving these key issues, and you'll likely notice a significant decline in your stress levels.

Another tool in your arsenal should be regular physical activity. Exercise isn't just good for your body; it's a potent stress reliever. Whether it's a morning swim, a noon yoga class, or a quick jog after work, find an activity that fits into your schedule and stick to it. The endorphins released during exercise can be just the ticket to keeping your stress levels under control.

Lastly, don't underestimate the power of a good night's sleep. Sleep is as crucial to your health as food and water, yet many entrepreneurs treat it as a luxury. Aim for 7-9 hours per night to optimise your health and reduce stress.

The Importance of Physical Health

It's no secret that maintaining an optimal level of physical health boosts your focus and energy levels, which can in turn, skyrocket your efficiency. This doesn't mean morphing into an ultra-marathoner or a fitness model – it means creating a balance where physical activity complements your work and your life.

Consider integrating exercise directly into your workday to make it a non-negotiable part of your routine. How about walking meetings? Not only do they help you fit exercise into a hectic schedule, but they can also boost creativity and engagement. Alternatively, if your workspace allows, why not try a standing desk or a treadmill desk?

Nutrition also plays a critical role in physical health. As tempting as it may be to power through the day on coffee and takeaways, proper nutrition is essential for maintaining high energy levels and overall health. Meal prepping can be a game-changer here. Spending a few hours every Sunday preparing meals can ensure you have healthy, nutritious food throughout the week, saving you time and helping you avoid the lure of less healthy options.

Lastly, regular check-ups aren't just for cars. A yearly physical exam will help you catch potential health issues before they become serious. Remember, as an entrepreneur, your health is your wealth.

Mindfulness and Emotional Health

Amid the hustle and bustle of running a business, it's easy to neglect your emotional health. However, maintaining an awareness of your emotional state and practicing mindfulness can enhance your decision-making skills, boost your creativity, and improve your relationships.

Start with mindfulness meditation. Just10 minutes a day can increase your concentration and decrease stress levels. There are plenty of apps that can guide you through the process, tailored to busy individuals who might only have a few minutes to spare.

Journaling is another powerful tool for emotional health. It can help you clarify your thoughts and feelings, understand yourself better, and reduce stress. Every night, try to jot down three things you were grateful for that day. This practice can shift your mindset from focusing on challenges to appreciating the positives in your life.

Lastly, don't overlook the value of emotional intelligence in leadership. Being able to understand and manage your emotions, and empathise with others, can lead to healthier workplace relationships and a more harmonious business environment. Consider reading up on emotional intelligence or taking workshops to improve these skills.

Remember, personal wellbeing isn't about keeping your head above water. It's about learning to surf the waves. As you implement these strategies, you'll not only enhance your own health and happiness but also set a powerful example for your team. They say the best leaders lead by example, and what better example to set than that of a balanced, healthy lifestyle?

Sustaining the Balance Long-Term

Regular Life Audits

As an entrepreneur, you're no stranger to the concept of audits in business – those thorough examinations that tell you how well your company is performing financially. But when was the last time you conducted an audit on your life? Regular life audits are crucial for ensuring that the balance you strive for doesn't just become a one-off achievement but a sustained reality.

Imagine a life audit as a personal quarterly review. Set aside a day every three months to reflect on different aspects of your life: your work achievements and setbacks, your personal relationships, your physical and mental health, and your personal goals. Are these in harmony, or is one area overpowering the others?

To perform a life audit, start by listing your priorities. What truly matters to you? Next, assess how much time and energy you are investing in each of these areas. You might find that while your business is thriving, your personal relationships or health may be suffering. This insight allows you to recalibrate and make informed decisions, much like you would adjust your business strategies after reviewing your company's quarterly financial reports.

Keep a journal or a digital record of these audits. Over time, these records will not only show you the areas where you've improved, but they will also highlight patterns or recurring challenges. This ongoing process ensures that you maintain a proactive stance towards balancing your life, rather than a reactive one.

Maintaining Flexibility

Flexibility might seem like a counter-intuitive suggestion in a discussion about balance. After all, isn't the whole idea to establish a firm structure? However, maintaining flexibility is key to long-term balance. It's about adopting a mindset that is resilient to the unexpected shifts in both your personal and professional life.

For instance, you might have a typical day planned out perfectly: a morning workout, key meetings lined up, and a family dinner in the evening. But what happens when an unexpected client request throws your schedule off balance? If you rigidly stick to your planned schedule, you risk escalating stress and dropping one of the balls you're juggling. Conversely, a flexible approach allows you to adapt your plans, perhaps by rescheduling the workout or shifting some meetings to accommodate the urgent client request.

This approach also applies to how you manage your team. Encouraging flexibility in work arrangements, such as remote work or flexible hours, can lead to higher productivity and better work-life balance for your team, which in turn benefits your business.

Flexibility doesn't mean living in a constant state of flux; rather, it's about having core priorities while also being able to adapt efficiently and effectively to the unexpected. It's akin to being a skilled surfer, riding the waves of entrepreneurism, ready to adjust your stance with the changing tides.

Engaging Support Networks

No entrepreneur is an island, even though it might feel that way sometimes. Sustaining work-life balance isn't just about what you can do alone but also about how well you leverage your support networks. These networks can be personal, like family and friends, or professional, such as mentors, peers, or a dedicated team.

Engaging these networks means more than just reaching out when things go awry. It involves regular interaction and involvement, ensuring that when you do need support, you're not making that call in a crisis. For example, regular catch-ups with mentors can provide you with a sounding board for your ideas and challenges. Meanwhile, family dinners or outings can help maintain strong personal relationships, providing you with a solid foundation and a respite from the pressures of business.

Moreover, don't overlook the power of peer support networks. Other entrepreneurs likely face similar challenges as you do. Forums, local business groups, or online communities can be invaluable spaces to share strategies, vent frustrations, and learn new approaches to maintaining balance.

Building and maintaining these networks require effort and time, but the return on investment is significant. They not only provide emotional or strategic support but also enhance your resilience, giving you a broader perspective and helping you navigate the complexities of entrepreneurial life.

In conclusion, sustaining work-life balance long-term is an ongoing process that requires regular evaluations, adaptability, and active engagement with your support networks. By incorporating these strategies into your routine, you ensure that maintaining balance becomes a part of your entrepreneurial journey, not just a distant goal. This approach not only enhances your personal well-being but ultimately contributes to the sustained success and health of your business.

RECAP AND ACTION ITEMS

You've just navigated through the essential components of balancing work and life, understanding how to integrate both, boosting your personal wellbeing, and sustaining this balance long-term. Now, it's time to transform these insights into actionable steps that can significantly enhance your productivity and personal satisfaction.

Firstly, let's address the myth of perfect balance. Remember, it's not about perfection but practicality. Start by setting clear boundaries for work and personal time. This week, experiment with specific start and end times for your workday. Communicate these changes to your team and family, ensuring they understand and respect your new boundaries.

Next, focus on your personal wellbeing. Could you incorporate one stress management technique into your routine? Whether it's meditation, a short walk, or a full workout, choose an activity that suits your lifestyle and schedule it just like a business meeting. Consistency here is crucial.

Also, never underestimate the power of physical health. A healthy body supports a sharp mind. This week, commit to three workout sessions and stick to them no matter what. Think of these sessions as investments in your business's biggest asset: you.

Mindfulness and emotional health are just as vital. Spend 10 minutes each day on a mindfulness exercise. It could be as simple as practicing deep breathing or jotting down things you're grateful for. These small practices can dramatically improve your emotional resilience.

For long-term balance, schedule a monthly life audit. Assess what's working and what isn't. Flexibility is your friend here; don't be afraid to tweak your strategies as your personal and professional life evolves.

Finally, lean on your support networks. Share your goals and struggles with a trusted friend or mentor. They can offer invaluable perspectives and keep you accountable.

By integrating these practices, you're not just surviving; you're thriving. Remember, the goal is to build a life that feels as good on the inside as it looks on the outside. Start small, be consistent, and watch how these changes positively impact your life and business.

10

SCALING YOUR SUCCESS

> "IF YOU WANT TO GO FAST, GO ALONE. IF YOU WANT TO GO FAR, GO TOGETHER." – AFRICAN PROVERB

Principles of Scaling

When to Scale

Knowing when to scale is akin to reading the weather before a sail. Time it right, and you catch the best winds that propel you swiftly forward; time it wrong, and you might find yourself battling a storm. As an entrepreneur, your business is your boat, and scaling is your voyage into deeper waters.

The first indicator that it's time to scale is when your current resources are consistently maximised yet demand continues to rise. This could mean your customer service team is overwhelmed, your inventory turnover is faster than you can replenish, or your servers are struggling under the load of web traffic. Essentially, if your current setup is bursting at the seams, it's time to consider scaling up.

Another sign is market readiness. If there's a clear demand not just locally but broader geographically, or if there are adjacent markets where your product or service could solve similar problems, these are green lights. However, it's crucial to back this up with solid data. Anecdotal evidence and gut feelings are valuable, but numbers don't lie. Conduct market research, analyse industry trends, and perhaps most importantly, listen to your existing customers—they're often the best barometers of potential success in new arenas.

Finally, ensure you have the right team to manage this growth. Scaling adds layers of complexity to operations, and having a team that's adaptable, skilled, and aligned with your vision is crucial. If you're confident in your team's ability to handle and drive growth, it might just be the right time to expand your horizons.

Scaling Strategies

Once you've decided that it's time to scale, how do you actually go about it? The strategies you choose can vary widely depending on your business model, industry, and specific goals, but there are a few common approaches that have been proven effective across multiple domains.

One popular strategy is scaling operations. This could involve opening new locations, expanding the size of existing facilities, or scaling up production capacity. It's all about increasing your ability to produce and deliver your product or service. However, operational scaling requires significant capital investment and careful planning to ensure that quality doesn't suffer as quantity increases.

Another strategy is scaling through technology. For many businesses, investing in technology can help automate processes, reduce costs, and increase output without necessarily expanding physical resources. Whether it's upgrading IT infrastructure, employing AI and machine learning for better customer service, or using online platforms for wider distribution, technology can be a powerful tool for scaling.

Franchising is another route, especially for businesses where the brand experience can be replicated at different locations. This allows for rapid expansion without the need to manage each new outlet directly. However, it requires a robust business model and brand that can be easily packaged and taught to others.

Each of these strategies has its own set of challenges and requires careful implementation. It's often wise to test small before going big—trial an approach in a limited scope to refine the strategy based on real-world feedback.

Risks and Rewards

Scaling is not without its perils. The potential rewards are significant—higher revenue, greater market share, and a stronger brand reputation. However, these come with risks that must be managed to avoid becoming another cautionary tale of expansion gone wrong.

One of the primary risks is overextension. In the rush to capitalize on perceived opportunities, it's possible to stretch your resources too thin. This can lead to compromised product quality, diminished customer service, and a stressed team that makes more mistakes. Financial overreach is another critical risk; pouring too much capital into expansion efforts without adequate returns can cripple a business.

Cultural dilution is a less obvious but equally dangerous risk. As businesses grow, maintaining a consistent company culture and ethos becomes challenging. This can affect employee morale and customer experience, undermining the very things that made the business successful initially.

However, with great risk comes great reward. Successfully scaled businesses can achieve economies of scale, reducing the per-unit cost of production and increasing overall profitability. Expansion also opens up new markets, offering more diverse revenue streams that can protect against economic downturns in any one region.

Moreover, scaling can enhance your business's attractiveness to potential investors. A proven capability to grow effectively increases confidence in your business's potential, making it easier to attract funding for further expansion.

In conclusion, scaling a business requires a delicate balance of timing, strategy, and risk management. It's about knowing when to push forward and when to consolidate gains. With thoughtful planning and execution, the act of scaling can unlock new levels of success and longevity for your business.

Implementing Growth Strategies

Diversification, market expansion, leveraging partnerships—these aren't just buzzwords; they are vital cogs in the engine driving your business towards greater success. Each element offers a unique advantage and, when implemented effectively, can substantially elevate the growth trajectory of your enterprise. Let's delve into how you can use these strategies to not just grow, but thrive.

Diversification

Think of diversification as your business's insurance policy against market volatility. It's about spreading your eggs across multiple baskets, reducing dependence on a single source of revenue which can be risky in an unpredictable business climate.

Start by evaluating your current offerings. What products or services have the highest margins? Which ones are underperforming? This analysis will guide you in understanding where opportunities for diversification exist. For instance, if you're running a software company that specialises in accounting tools, consider branching into related areas such as payroll processing or financial compliance.

However, diversification isn't just about adding new products or services—it's also about innovation and adaptation. Explore how you can modify existing products to open up new markets. Perhaps a slight alteration could make one of your products suitable for an entirely different industry or consumer segment.

Another aspect is geographical diversification. Expanding into new territories can open up fresh streams of revenue and spread risk. But remember, this involves extensive market research to understand local consumer behaviour, regulatory requirements, and potential barriers to entry.

Lastly, consider diversification through acquisition. Buying a company that complements or enhances your existing operations can be a quick way to diversify. It not only adds to your capabilities and offerings but might also bring new customer bases, talented employees, and valuable intellectual property.

Market Expansion

Expanding into new markets is thrilling, but it's fraught with challenges. It demands a deep understanding of the new market's culture, needs, and regulations. Whether you're looking at international markets or different demographic segments in your current region, the key is to tailor your approach to fit the local preferences and conditions.

Begin by identifying markets with the highest potential for your products or services. Look for regions where demand is growing but supply is not yet saturated. Tools like market analysis reports, economic forecasts, and demographic studies can be invaluable here.

Once you've pinpointed a target market, immerse yourself in understanding its nuances. What are the local consumer trends? How do competitors operate here? What are the cultural nuances that could affect the adoption of your product? For example, if you are expanding from the UK to Asia, consider cultural preferences and how they might impact your product usage.

Cultural adaptation of your marketing strategies is also crucial. This could mean modifying your advertising campaigns to resonate with local values or adjusting your product packaging to appeal to local tastes. Remember, what works in one market might not work in another.

Building a local presence can greatly aid in market expansion. This might involve setting up a physical office or store, or building partnerships with local businesses and influencers to increase brand visibility and credibility.

Leveraging Partnerships

Partnerships can be a powerful tool to accelerate growth, allowing you to share resources, tap into new customer bases, and enhance your market credibility. The key is choosing the right partners whose vision aligns with yours and whose strengths complement your weaknesses.

Start by identifying potential partners. These could be businesses that offer complementary products or services, or those that have a strong presence in a market you're trying to enter. When evaluating potential partners, consider factors such as their market reputation, customer base, operational strengths, and strategic fit with your business.

Once you've identified a suitable partner, focus on building a relationship based on transparency and mutual benefit. Clearly define the objectives and expectations of the partnership. What does each party bring to the table? How will profits and costs be shared? How will decisions be made?

Effective collaboration is crucial. This might involve co-developing products, cross-promoting services, or jointly hosting events. Each partner's strengths should be leveraged to maximise the benefits of the partnership. For instance, if your partner has an extensive distribution network, you might use this to increase the reach of your products.

Regularly review the partnership to ensure it remains mutually beneficial. Set up meetings to discuss challenges and opportunities, and adjust your strategy as needed to keep the partnership productive and aligned with changing market conditions.

By effectively implementing these growth strategies—diversification, market expansion, leveraging partnerships—you not only increase your business's footprint but also enhance its resilience against economic shifts. Each strategy opens up new avenues for revenue and growth, ensuring that your business not only grows but does so sustainably and robustly in the face of ever-evolving market dynamics.

Sustaining Growth

Innovation as a Habit

In the constantly evolving marketplace, resting on your laurels is the quickest path to obsolescence. As a business owner, you know that what worked yesterday might not suffice today, and almost certainly won't tomorrow. Embracing innovation not as a one-off project but as a daily habit can be your game-changer.

Think of innovation less as product development and more as problem-solving. Every day brings new challenges and opportunities to improve, whether that's enhancing your product, streamlining your services, or optimising internal processes. Encourage your team to think in terms of solutions rather than tasks. A simple shift in mindset from 'completing' to 'improving' can lead to significant enhancements in how your business operates.

One effective method to institutionalise innovation is through regular brainstorming sessions. These shouldn't be staid, scheduled affairs that everyone dreads. Make them quick, impromptu, and even fun. Throw a challenge to the team and give them a short time to come up with as many solutions as possible. This not only generates ideas but also cultivates an atmosphere where creativity is valued and rewarded.

Moreover, consider setting aside a small percentage of time and resources for experimentation. Google famously allows its employees to spend 20% of their time on side projects, many of which have gone on to become core services. While you might not be Google, the principle holds: a little leeway to explore can lead to significant business innovations.

Managing Larger Teams

As your enterprise grows, so does your team. And while it's thrilling to see your business scale, managing an expanding team presents a new set of challenges. Communication lines that were once direct become complex, and the close-knit culture you've nurtured may start to dilute.

The key here is not just to manage, but to lead. As your team grows, your leadership style should evolve from being involved in every decision to empowering others to make those decisions. This transition can be tough, but it's vital for sustainable growth.

Start by establishing clear structures and roles within the team. Ambiguity can lead to inefficiencies and frustration. Each member of your team should know their responsibilities and how they contribute to the wider business goals.

Training and development play a crucial role here. Invest in your team's growth, not just for their individual careers but for the benefit of the business.

Skilled, knowledgeable teams are not only more productive but also more motivated and engaged.

Another aspect to consider is fostering a strong culture. As teams grow, the intimate startup vibe can get lost. Keep the lines of communication open and maintain those rituals that define your company's culture—be it weekly catch-ups, team outings, or open feedback sessions. A strong culture can act as the glue that holds your team together as it expands.

Staying Competitive in a Changing Market

The market waits for no one. Changes in technology, consumer behaviour, and regulatory environments can happen in the blink of an eye. To sustain growth, you need to not just keep up but stay ahead.

Continuous market research is your radar in navigating these waters. It's not enough to know your audience; you must also understand the ecosystem your business operates in. This includes keeping tabs on competitors, changes in consumer preferences, and emerging industry trends. Equip yourself with this knowledge, and you'll be better positioned to anticipate market shifts rather than just react to them.

Adaptability is your next tool. Once you have the information, the real challenge is how quickly and effectively you can adapt. This might mean pivoting your business model, as Netflix did when it moved from DVD rentals to streaming, or it could be a subtle shift in marketing strategy to appeal to a new demographic.

Lastly, leverage technology. In an age where tech is king, using the right tools can give you a significant competitive edge. Whether it's advanced analytics to predict consumer behaviour, automation tools to enhance productivity, or cutting-edge marketing platforms to reach new audiences, technology can be a catalyst for sustaining growth.

In conclusion, sustaining growth is about embedding innovation into your daily routine, scaling your leadership as your team grows, and staying agile in a dynamic market environment. By focusing on these areas, you ensure that your business not only grows but thrives and adapts, regardless of what the future holds.

RECAP AND ACTION ITEMS

By now, you've thoroughly explored the multifaceted approach to scaling your business. From pinpointing the optimal moment for growth, through strategizing your expansion, to maintaining your competitive edge, each phase carries its unique set of challenges and opportunities.

Firstly, remember that scaling is not merely about getting bigger, but getting better. It's about smart growth that aligns with your long-term vision. Ask yourself not just when to scale, but why. Is your business truly ready to expand, or are there foundational improvements needed first? Keep these questions at the forefront to ensure your growth is sustainable and not just a fleeting surge.

Moving forward, you've delved into diversification, market expansion, and leveraging partnerships. These are powerful strategies, but they require careful implementation. Diversification should not dilute your brand but enrich it. As you consider entering new markets, do thorough research to understand cultural nuances and customer needs. Partnerships should be symbiotic, not parasitic, enhancing both your capabilities and your partners'.

Lastly, sustaining growth is an ongoing process. Infuse innovation into your company culture to keep your team motivated and your products or services fresh. Managing larger teams will require you to delegate effectively and invest in leadership development within your ranks. Staying competitive means staying relevant, so keep your finger on the pulse of industry trends and shifts in consumer behaviour.

Action Steps:

1. Conduct a scalability audit: Evaluate your current operations, resources, and market conditions to assess readiness for scaling

2. Develop a growth strategy plan: Outline specific steps for diversification, market expansion, and partnership opportunities

3. Create an innovation agenda: Schedule regular brainstorming sessions and encourage a culture of creativity and experimentation

4. Leadership training: Invest in training programmes for your team leaders to ensure they are equipped to manage growing teams

5. Stay informed: Dedicate time each week to study market trends and emerging technologies in your industry.

By systematically following these steps, you'll not only scale your business effectively but also ensure it thrives in a competitive landscape. Remember, the journey of scaling is not a sprint but a marathon, requiring persistence, adaptability, and strategic foresight.

11

EMBRACING THE JOURNEY: A CALL TO ACTION

As you reach the final pages of this transformative guide, take a moment to reflect on the journey you've embarked upon. The principles and strategies shared throughout this book are designed to equip you with the tools to enhance your productivity and revolutionise your daily routine. But remember, the true measure of these insights is not only in their application but in the sustainable changes they foster in both your professional and personal life.

Productivity is not simply about doing more in less time; it's about making each moment truly count. It's about creating a life that balances achievement with fulfilment, and progress with peace. This book has laid out a framework to help you build that kind of life. The strategies discussed have the potential to propel you towards not only greater efficiency but also a deeper sense of purpose. Yet, the end of this book is not the end of your journey—it is, in fact, a new beginning. A starting point from which you can launch into a future where your dreams and daily actions align more closely than ever before.

The world we live in today is busier and more demanding than ever. Distractions are plentiful, and the pressure to perform can be overwhelming. It's easy to feel lost in the shuffle, as though your deepest goals and passions must be set aside for the sake of immediate demands. However, you hold the power to reshape your life's narrative. By mastering self-discipline, optimising your workspace, and leveraging technology, you've taken vital steps towards a more intentional and rewarding existence.

Yet, as you know, knowledge alone is not enough. Action is the bridge between intention and realisation. It is through purpose-driven action that your goals will move from the realm of possibility to the realm of reality. Consider this book your roadmap. Each chapter has provided you with key insights and actionable steps. Now, it is up to you to implement them consistently, refining and adapting as you go.

But what happens when challenges arise? As you've learned, the path to peak productivity is not without obstacles. There will be days when motivation fades and your carefully crafted routines falter. In those moments, remember why you started this journey. Revisit your goals—not just the immediate ones, but the larger aspirations that fuel your ambition. Let them remind you that each step, no matter how small, is a vital part of the larger journey towards success and satisfaction.

Additionally, no journey worth taking is meant to be travelled alone. Surround yourself with a community of like-minded individuals—those who encourage, challenge, and inspire you to rise even when you stumble. Professional guidance is always available to help you navigate particularly difficult terrain or to accelerate your progress when you're ready to reach the next level.

If you find yourself seeking more personalised advice or need specific guidance tailored to your unique situation, don't hesitate to reach out. You can connect with Neil and Ian on LinkedIn, where they are available to offer advice, share insights, and provide professional coaching that can help you refine your productivity techniques, enhance your time management skills, or develop resilience in the face of professional pressures.

EMBRACING THE JOURNEY: A CALL TO ACTION

As you move forward, keep in mind that productivity is not a destination but an ongoing journey. It is an ever-evolving practice that adapts to your growing needs and changing circumstances. Stay curious, stay committed, and, most importantly, remain open to the transformations that await.

Finally, as we conclude, remember that the essence of productivity lies in making space for what truly matters. It's about clearing away the unnecessary to allow the essential to shine through. It is about not just doing more, but being more—more present, more engaged, and more fulfilled.

Now, as you set this book aside and step back into your life, take with you not only the lessons learned but the excitement for what lies ahead. Your journey towards exceptional productivity and personal growth is just beginning, and the best is yet to come.

Thank you for allowing this book to be part of your journey. Here's to your continued success and the many achievements that await you. Remember, the path to productivity is an ongoing, ever-rewarding pursuit—embrace it fully, and let it elevate you to heights you never thought possible.

www.ingramcontent.com/pod-product-compliance
Lightning Source LLC
Chambersburg PA
CBHW071059240526
45471CB00016B/2164